Cooking With Hugh

By: Hugh A. Hardy, Jr.

Sponsored by:

Carroll's Sausage & Meats, Inc.

For more information about the
"Cooking With Hugh" show
or
Carroll's Sausage & Meats:

Tel: 229-776-2628
Fax: 229-776-9079
Email: info@cookingwithhugh.com

Be sure to visit our website:
www.cookingwithhugh.com

FATHER
&
SON
PUBLISHING, INC.
4909 N. Monroe Street • Tallahassee, Florida 32303
http://www.fatherson.com email lance @fatherson.com
800-741-2712

Introduction

I was born in Ashburn, Georgia on August 6, 1974. I grew up on my Granddad's farm about 9 miles out of town in the country. Farming was my family's life and living. We grew peanuts, corn, soybeans, watermelons, etc. We also had a lot of cows.

I learned how to work at a very young age. I remember driving a tractor when I was just 4 years old. I had to work pretty much everyday after school. I can still remember picking peanuts sometimes until 11:00 pm, even on school nights. I really learned how to appreciate life growing up on a farm.

We always had some of the best home-cooking around. My Mom and Granny were great cooks. A good home-cooked meal was always so good after a long day in the field. Fried chicken, turnip greens, peas, mashed potatoes, and homemade biscuits were my favorites. My Granny made some dang good chicken and dumplings, too. Thanks to the good Lord, we always had plenty to eat. Over the years, I learned how to cook from my Mom.

My parents quit farming when I was 15 years old. At age 16, I went to work for a local grocery store part-time after school. I really enjoyed working with the public; it paid off, because that's what I do now for a living.

In February 2001 I purchased Carroll's Sausage & Meats along with the help of a partner. Soon after we bought the business, I bought out my partner and made a go of it alone. Carroll's Sausage has truly been a blessing to me. Now I have three stores and a great team of employees who have all contributed to my success.

My dream has always been to have my own cooking show. With some help from friends, I've been able to see that dream come true. "Cooking With Hugh" has aired on WALB-10, FOX 31, and WSST-55. Wow, sometimes I can't believe it myself…some poor ole country boy hosting a cooking show. My favorite segment is Pastor Mike McPherson's "Strength for Today". It touches my heart and I know it touches others as well (thank you Brother Mike).

My life hasn't always been so wonderful. I've had my share of ups and downs, but through it all, God never left my side. He continues to bless me even though I am not a perfect person.

I really hope you enjoy this cookbook and if you're ever in my area, Sycamore, Sylvester, or Albany, Georgia, stop by Carroll's Sausage & Meats and get some sausage…just like grandpa used to make.

Hugh A. Hardy, Jr

Foreword

***Proverbs 22:1* (MSG)** A sterling reputation is better than striking it rich; a gracious spirit is better than money in the bank.

A good reputation is valuable. King Solomon of ancient Israel stated, "A good name is more desirable than great riches."

Where does a good reputation come from?

Good reputation is what we see, character is what lies under the surface and produces it. For instance, when baking a strawberry cake, many ingredients are mixed together, placed in an oven and baked, and then the icing is put on it. The baked cake presents itself as something that is seen and to be desired, however it is the single ingredients added together that make the cake what it is.

So it is with a man's reputation. What you see is the shadow of what lies underneath the surface. Good character is what produces a sterling reputation.

The ingredients of good character might be described in the following ways:

For the Boy Scout, good character is described this way: trustworthy, loyal, helpful, friendly, courteous, kind, obedient, cheerful, thrifty, brave, clean, and reverent.

For the Christian, good character is described this way: love, joy, peace, patience, kindness, goodness, faithfulness, gentleness, self control.

For the Successful Individual, good character is

described as being considerate, confident, consistent, caring, controlled, courageous, conscientious, creative, and Christ-like.

Considering the fact that words communicate the impression that we get from observing someone, it is my conviction that Hugh Hardy has set his goals in life high and as a result of his good character, God is adding the benefits of good character to his life.

Hugh Hardy has a good reputation because he is a good person; He is a good person because he has sterling character.

Fame is a vapor,
Popularity is an accident,
Riches take wings,
Only one thing endures,
Character.

Strength Thought for Today

Godly character produces a Sterling reputation!

by Brother Mike McPherson

TABLE OF CONTENTS

A Country Boy
An original poem by "Rooster" the dishwasher

I don't claim to be rich,
And I shore ain't smart,
But being a country boy,
Makes a fellow feel good in his heart.

I was born in the backwoods,
Reared on cornbread and peas,
Taught to sleep with the dog,
And help him knock off fleas.

I can't plow a mule,
I can't even shuck an ear of corn,
But I've been fed syrup and biscuits,
Ever since I was born.

I ain't dug a ditch to China,
Nor sailed the ocean blue,
But live in the country,
That's what I want to do.

I don't claim to be rich,
And I shore ain't smart,
But being a country boy,
Makes a fellow feel good in his heart.

Appetizers, Dips, Pickles, Jellies and Preserves

Index

Favorite Recipes:

Title   Page Number

_____

_____

_____

_____

_____

_____

_____

_____

_____

_____

_____

_____

_____

_____

_____

Cheesestraws

6   Cups Sharp Cheese, Grated
1½   Cups Butter
3½ Cups Self-Rising Flour
Tabasco Sauce (amount depends on taste)

Let grated cheese soften, add butter, mix well. Gradually add flour and Tabasco sauce to cheese mixture. Blend until smooth (using food processor works great). Using cookie press, press out dough in long straws on greased baking sheet. Bake in preheated 350 degree oven for 15 to 20 minutes until lightly browned. Do not over bake. Cut straws into 2 inch pieces while still hot.

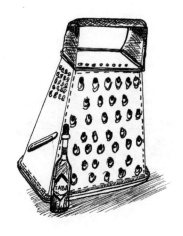

Cheesy Bacon Potato Skins

2	**Large Potatoes, Baked**
1	**Cup Cheddar Cheese, Shredded**
½	**Cup Bacon Bits**
½	**Cup Sour Cream**

Cut each baked potato in half lengthwise. Scoop out most of the potato. Cut each half in half again lengthwise, should have four strips. Place slices on baking sheet, sprinkle bacon bits evenly in each slice, top with shredded cheese. Bake at 350 degrees for 10 minutes or until skins are crispy and cheese is melted. Serve with sour cream for dipping.

Chex Party Mix

2½	**Cups Corn Chex Cereal**
2½	**Cups Rice Chex Cereal**
2½	**Cups Wheat Chex Cereal**
1	**Cup Salted Mixed Nuts**
½	**Cup Butter**
1½	**Tablespoon Worcestershire Sauce**
1	**Teaspoon Seasoned Salt**

Heat butter in a large shallow roasting pan in preheated 350 degree oven until butter melts. Remove from oven, stir in Worcestershire sauce and seasoned salt. Add cereals and nuts and mix until everything is completely coated. Return to oven and heat about one hour, stirring every 15 minutes. Spread on paper towel to cool, store in airtight container.

Deviled Eggs

9   Eggs, Hard Boiled, Peeled
4   Tablespoons Mayonnaise
2   Tablespoons Pickle Relish
1   Teaspoon Yellow Mustard
Paprika
Salt and Pepper to Taste

Cut boiled eggs in half lengthwise. Remove yolks. Combine yolks, one egg white, mayonnaise, relish, mustard, salt and pepper. Mix well. Spoon into yolks, sprinkle with paprika if desired.

Ham Roll-Ups

1	**Package Sliced Cooked Ham** (16 ounce)
1	**Package Cream Cheese** (8 ounce), **Softened**
4	**Tablespoons Mayonnaise**
2	**Tablespoons Onion, Chopped Very Fine**
1	**Tablespoon Chives**

Mix cream cheese, mayonnaise, onion and chives together. Spread mixture on one side of each slice of ham. Roll ham jelly roll style, cover and chill in refrigerator. After chilled, slice before serving.

Hint: After rolled, wrap tightly in plastic wrap before refrigerating.

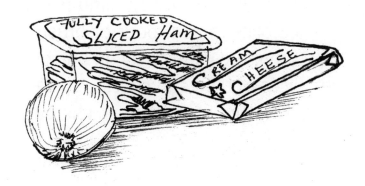

Ham Rolls

1	**Cup Butter**
1/4	**Cup Onion, Chopped**
3	**Tablespoons Yellow Mustard**
2	**Tablespoons Poppy Seeds**
2	**Tablespoons Worcestershire Sauce**
2	**Packages Small Dinner Rolls** (in aluminum pan)

Thin Sliced Ham
Cheese, Sliced

Heat butter and onions in microwave safe bowl until butter is melted and onions are tender. Add mustard, Worcestershire sauce, and poppy seeds, mixing well. Make sure thoroughly heated. Leave rolls connected, but cut rolls in half, creating a large top and bottom slice. Line original dinner roll pan with aluminum foil, place bottom slice back in pan, pour or brush poppy seed butter mixture generously on bottom slice. Top with slices of ham and cheese. Spread more poppy seed butter mixture over cheese. Place

---

cheese. If still some butter remaining, pour over tops of rolls. Cover rolls with aluminum foil, bake in preheated 350 degree oven for about 20 minutes. Easy to remove from pan since lined with foil — open foil and cut individual rolls with electric knife.

Oyster Cracker Snacks

1	**Envelope Hidden Valley Original Buttermilk Dressing Mix**
1	**Teaspoon Dill Weed**
½	**Teaspoon Garlic Powder**
½	**Teaspoon Lemon Pepper**
2	**Boxes Oyster Crackers** (12 ounce)
1	**Cup Vegetable Oil**

Mix dressing mix, dill weed, garlic powder and lemon pepper together. Place oyster crackers in a large container, sprinkle dressing mixture over crackers, gently stir. Pour vegetable oil over crackers. Seal container, shake well. Let crackers set for awhile on counter, turning container over every 30 minutes or so, until oil has been absorbed.

Cheese Ball

8   Ounces Cream Cheese
2   Tablespoons Mayonnaise
½   Teaspoon Worcestershire Sauce
1   Teaspoon Onion, Finely Chopped
1   Tablespoon Olives, Finely Chopped
1   Jar Dried Beef (2½ ounce), Finely
         Chopped
Coarse Ground Black Pepper

Let cream cheese get to room temperature, then mix all ingredients together, except black pepper. Shape into a ball, roll in black pepper, covering outside of cheese ball. Serve with several different kinds of crackers.

Sausage Balls

1	**Pound Carroll's Pan Sausage,** **(Medium or Hot)**
1	**Pound Sharp Cheese, Grated**
3	**Cups Biscuit Mix**

Mix all ingredients together and form into small balls. Bake at 400 degrees for 10 minutes. May be frozen before or after baking.

Sausage Turnovers

Carroll's Pan Sausage,
      (Mild, Medium or Hot), Browned
Canned Biscuits
      (or Frozen Biscuits that have thawed)
Cheddar Cheese, Grated

Roll each biscuit into a 4 inch circle. Place a spoonful of cooked sausage in middle of biscuit circle, sprinkle with cheese, fold dough over, seal edges with fork. Bake in a 400 degree oven for 10 minutes, or until browned.

Sugar Peanuts

2	**Cups Raw Peanuts** (with skins)
I	**Cup Sugar**
½	**Cup Water**

Combine sugar and water in a heavy pot, cook over medium heat until sugar dissolves turning into a syrup. Add peanuts and continue cooking, stirring frequently, until syrup starts to sugar, forming sugar crystals on peanuts. When peanuts are completely coated with sugar crystals and no syrup is left in pan, pour onto an ungreased cookie sheet that has been lined with foil. Spread so that peanuts are separated. Bake at 300 degrees for about 15 to 20 minutes, stirring every five minutes or so to keep peanuts separated. Cool completely, seal in air tight container.

Sweet & Sour Cocktail Wieners

1-2	**Pound Small Cocktail Wieners**
½	**Cup Chili Sauce**
½	**Cup Grape Jelly**
½	**Tablespoon Yellow Mustard**
1	**Teaspoon Lemon Juice**
1	**Can Pineapple Chunks,**
	(16 - 20 ounce), Drained

Combine chili sauce, jelly, mustard and lemon juice in large skillet, mix well, add wieners and pineapple chunks. Heat to boiling, reduce heat and simmer 15 minutes, Stirring occasionally. Serve warm.

Cream Dill Dip

½   **Cup Mayonnaise**
½   **Cup Sour Cream**
2   **Tablespoons Onion, Finely Chopped**
1   **Teaspoon Dill**
¼   **Teaspoon Salt**

Combine all ingredients, mix well. Chill — flavor best if chilled overnight. If too thick, can add milk, a teaspoonful at a time. Serve with raw vegetables.

Spinach Bacon Dip

1   **Pound Velveeta Cheese, Cubed**
1   **Package Frozen Chopped Spinach**
    (10 ounce) Thawed and Drained
4   **Ounces Cream Cheese**
1   **Can Ro-Tel Tomatoes and**
    Green Chillies (10 ounce)
8   **Slices Bacon, Crisply Cooked,**
    Drained and Crumbled

Place cubed Velveeta in a large microwave safe dish, add thawed and drained spinach, cream cheese and Ro-Tel. Microwave at high heat 3 minutes stirring often. Continue to heat in microwave, stirring every 30 seconds or so until Velveeta and cream cheese are completely melted and mixture is well blended. Serve hot with tortilla chips, bread cubes or fresh vegetables.

Dried Beef Dip

1½   **Cups Sour Cream**
1½   **Cups Mayonnaise**
¼   **Cups Onion, Finely Chopped**
1   **Tablespoon Dried Parsley**
      (can use fresh chopped)
1   **Tablespoon Dill Weed**
1   **Jar Dried Beef** (2½ ounce)

Coarsely chop or cut up dried beef. Mix all other ingredients well, add dried beef, refrigerate at least overnight. Serve with chips or crackers.

Chipped Beef Dip

1	**Cup Sour Cream**
8	**Ounce Package Cream Cheese**
1	**Jar Dried Beef** (2½ ounce), **Finely Chopped**
1–2	**Dashes Tabasco Sauce**
1	**Teaspoon Worcestershire Sauce**
¼–½	**Teaspoon Garlic Powder**

Blend sour cream and softened cream cheese together. Add dried beef, Tabasco, Worcestershire Sauce and garlic powder. Cook in oven or in microwave until heated thoroughly. Serve hot with crackers or chips.

Hot Cheese Dip

2	Cups Sour Cream
8	Ounce Package Cream Cheese
½	Small Onion, Finely Chopped
1	Jar Dried Beef (2½ ounce), Finely Chopped
1½	Teaspoon Worcestershire Sauce
1	Teaspoon Garlic Powder
¼	Teaspoon Lawrey Seasoning
½	Cup Pecans, Chopped

Blend sour cream and softened cream cheese together. Add onion, dried beef, Worcestershire Sauce, garlic powder and Lawrey seasoning. Place in shallow baking dish, top with chopped pecans, cover with foil — bake at 350 degrees for 20 minutes, remove foil, bake additional 10 minutes.

Fruit Dip

1   **Cup Sour Cream**
1-2 **Tablespoons Brown Sugar**

Combine sugar and sour cream, mix well. Chill, stir before serving to make sure that sugar has dissolved completely. Serve with fresh fruit, cut into bite size pieces.

Zippy Mexican Dip

1   **Pound Carroll's Pan Sausage**
     (Medium or Hot)
1   **Can Ro-Tel Tomatoes and**
     Green Chillies *(10 ounce)*
1   **Pound Velveeta Cheese, Cubed**

Brown sausage, drain. Melt Velveeta in the microwave in a microwave safe dish at medium heat,
stirring often. Add Ro-tel contents to cheese,
continue to heat in microwave, stirring every 30
seconds or so until mixed well. Stir in browned
sausage. Serve hot with chips.

Easy Sausage Dip

1   **Pound Carroll's Pan Sausage**
    (Medium or Hot)
1   **Can Ro-Tel Tomatoes and**
    Green Chillies (10 ounce)
8   **Ounces Cream Cheese**

Brown sausage, drain. Heat cream cheese and Ro-tel contents in the microwave in a microwave safe dish at medium heat, for about 3 minutes stirring often. Continue to heat in microwave, stirring every 30 seconds or so until mixed well. Stir in browned sausage. Serve hot with tortilla chips.

Peach Pickles

8	Pounds Small Peaches, Peeled
3	Pounds Sugar
4	Sticks Cinnamon
2	Tablespoons Whole Cloves, Crushed
1	Tablespoon Fresh Ginger
1	Quart Water

Wash and peel peaches. (To prevent darkening, sprinkle peaches with lemon, orange or pineapple juice or a commercial anti-darkening preparation, such as Fruit-Fresh). Heat sugar and vinegar in a large sauce pot until sugar has dissolved. Boil additional 5 minutes. Add spices that have been tied into a cheesecloth bag into boiling syrup. Gently drop peaches into boiling sugar/vinegar syrup and cook until peaches can be easily pierced with a fork. Remove sauce pan from heat and allow peaches to sit in pickling syrup overnight.

PEACH PICKLES (continued)

Next day, bring peaches and syrup mixture back to a boil then carefully pack peaches into hot jars, filling jars with sugar/vinegar syrup, but leaving ¼ inch head room. Remove air bubbles from each jar by running a non-metallic spatula around inside each jar between the peaches and the jar. Wipe mouth of jar with clean towel, removing any syrup that may have dropped on jar. Seal jar with jar flats and rings, hand tightening only. Process jars for 20 minutes in a boiling water bath. Yield: about 3 quarts.

Fried Dill Pickles

½	**Cup Self-Rising Corn Meal Mix**
¼	**Cup Corn Starch**
¼	**Cups Self-Rising Flour**
½	**Cup Water**
1	**Egg, Slightly Beaten**
1	**Jar Dill Pickles, Drained**

Sliced Round, In Strips, or Wedges

Combine corn starch, corn meal mix and flour. Add water and beaten egg. Mix until smooth. Add dill pickles that have been drained and blotted dry between paper towels. Drop into medium hot grease (375 degrees), cook until golden brown, about 2 to 3 minutes on each side. Great as batter for tomatoes, onions, and other vegetables.

Strawberry-Fig Preserves

3   **Cups Figs, Peeled**
3   **Cups Sugar**
1   **Package Strawberry Jello** (3 ounce)
1   **Teaspoon Lemon Juice**

Combine all ingredients, bring to a boil, reduce heat and simmer 30 minutes. Pour into hot, sterilized jars, leaving ½ inch headspace, seal with jar flat and ring.

Mango Salsa

2	**Jars Sliced Mangos, Drained And Chopped, Reserve Juice**
½	**Cup Red Onions**
½	**Cup Celery**
½	**Cup Bell Pepper, Red, Chopped Jalapeño Pepper, Seeded and Sliced**
½	**Cup Bell Pepper, Yellow, Chopped Cilantro**

Stir all ingredients listed above together, add just enough mango juice to moisten. Cover and refrigerate overnight. Serve over fish taco or with crackers.

(Special thanks to Rachel Day)

Bacon-Wrapped Mushroom Caps

12-15 **Fresh, Whole Mushrooms, Wiped Clean**

12-15 **Fresh, Whole Grape Tomatoes, Cleaned**

½ **Pound Bacon**

¼ **Cup Italian Dressing**

Salt and pepper

Pop stems out of mushrooms. Place one grape tomato in base of each mushroom cap. Cut bacon slices in half and wrap a half slice of bacon around mushroom and tomato. Repeat for all mushrooms and tomatoes. Drizzle with Italian dressing and sprinkle with salt and pepper. Bake at 400 degrees for 15 to 20 minutes or until bacon is crisp.

Barbeque Sausage Balls

1	**Pound Carroll's Pan Sausage**
1	**Slightly Beaten Egg**
½	**Teaspoon Celery Salt**
½	**Cup Bread Crumbs**

Combine ingredients and shape into bite-sized balls. Brown gently on all sides in an ungreased skillet. Remove and place into casserole dish.

Sauce

½ **Cup Ketchup**

2 **Tablespoons Brown Sugar**

1 **Tablespoon Vinegar**

1 **Tablespoon Soy Sauce**

Combine ingredients and pour over meat. May use bottled barbeque sauce instead.

Cover and bake at 350 degrees for 30 minutes, stirring occasionally.

Stuffed Mushrooms

2 Pounds Fresh Mushrooms, Wiped Clean
1 Pound Carroll's Pan Sausage
½ Small Onion, Finely Diced
1 Box Italian Breadcrumbs
1 (8 Ounce) **Package Cream Cheese**
1 Stick Butter, Melted
½ Cup Shredded Cheddar Cheese

Brown sausage and onion over medium-high heat until meat is done. Remove stems from mushrooms and soak caps in melted butter. Chop stems and add to cooked sausage. Add all other bread crumbs and cream cheese and mix well. Place in casserole dish and bake covered at 350 degrees for 20 minutes. Uncover, sprinkle with cheese, and bake for 5 more minutes.

Cooking With Hugh

Salads,
Salad Dressings,
Sauces, Glazes
and Soups

Index

Favorite Recipes:

Title   Page Number

_____

_____

_____

_____

_____

_____

_____

_____

_____

_____

_____

_____

_____

_____

_____

_____

Carrot Raisin Salad

8-10   **Carrots, Shredded**

1   **Can Crushed Pineapple** (8 ounce), **Drained**

½   **Cup Raisins**

¼   **Cup Mayonnaise**

1   **Teaspoon Sugar**

Mix all ingredients together.
Chill and serve.

Apple Salad

Dressing for apple salad:
**Pineapple Juice (drained from 1 can
        crushed pineapple)**
½   **Cup Sugar**
1   **Tablespoon Flour**
1   **Egg**
2   **Tablespoons Apple Cider Vinegar**

Pineapple juice from one (8 ounce) can crushed pineapple. Combine flour and sugar; mix well. Beat egg; add to flour/sugar. Add vinegar and reserved pineapple juice. Cook in microwave 2 minutes on high until thickened, stirring every 30 seconds. Cool completely.

1   **Carton Whipped Topping** (8 ounce)
4   **Cups** (1 pound) **Red Delicious Apples,
        Cubed, <u>Unpeeled</u>**
1   **Cup Salted Shelled Peanuts**
1   **Can Crushed Pineapple, Drained**
        (8 ounce) (juice used in dressing)

APPLE SALAD (continued)

Pour cooled dressing over mixture of apples, pineapple and peanuts. Fold in whipped topping. Sprinkle with additional peanuts for garnish. Refrigerate until ready to serve.

Layered Lettuce Salad

1	**Head Of Lettuce, Broken Into Pieces**
½	**Cup Onion, Chopped**
½	**Cup Bell Pepper, Chopped**
½	**Cup Celery, Chopped**
1	**Can Young Early Peas** (15 ounce)
1	**Cup Mayonnaise**
2	**Tablespoons Sugar**
1	**Teaspoon Salt**
½	**Cup Parmesan Cheese, Grated**
½	**Cup Cheddar Cheese, Shredded**

Bacon, Cooked and Crumbled

Layer half of lettuce, onions, bell pepper, celery and peas in a glass trifle bowl. Repeat layers. Cover last layer (which should be peas) with mayonnaise (may need more than one cup) completely sealing vegetables. Sprinkle mayonnaise with sugar and salt, then Parmesan cheese. Garnish with cheese and bacon. Cover with plastic wrap and refrigerate over night. Can also add layers of water chestnuts and/or carrots.

Lime Congealed Salad

1	**Cup Water**
1	**Can Crushed Pineapple** (8 ounce), **Drained**
1/2	**Cup Miniature Marshmallows**
1	**Package Lime Jell-O** (3 ounce)
1	**Package Cream Cheese** (3 ounce), **Softened**
1/2	**Cup Pecans, Chopped**

Heat water and pineapple juice in microwave until boiling, add marshmallows, stirring frequently until marshmallows melt. Add Jell-O to water/juice mixture, stir until Jell-O completely dissolves, place in refrigerator until soft set. Meanwhile, mix pineapple and chopped nuts in softened cream cheese. Add cream cheese mixture to soft set Jell-O, mixing well. Refrigerate until completely set.

Potato Salad

6	**Medium Potatoes**
3	**Eggs, Hard Boiled, Chopped**
½	**Cups Mayonnaise**
¼	**Cup Pickle Relish, Sweet or Dill**
¼	**Cup Onion, Chopped**
1	**Tablespoon Yellow Mustard**

Salt and Pepper to Taste

Peel potatoes, cut into 1-inch cubes. Cover potatoes with water in a large saucepan, bring to a boil. Cook potatoes until tender (cracks when fork inserted). Drain. Add eggs, mayonnaise, relish, onion, mustard, salt and pepper to potatoes. Mix gently. Great served warm or cold.

Broccoli Cauliflower Salad

1   **Cup Sour Cream**
1   **Cup Mayonnaise**
1   **Package Hidden Valley Ranch original Salad Dressing Mix**
    (.4 ounces)
1   **Small Bunch Broccoli** (cut into bite size)
1   **Small Head Cauliflower** (cut into bite size)
1   **Can Small Green Peas, Drained**
    (8½ ounces)
1   **Small Onion, Chopped**
1   **Carrot, Sliced thin**
1   **Jar Bacon Bits** (3¼ ounces)
1   **Can Water Chesnuts, (8 ounces) Drained and Sliced - Optional**
1   **Cup Cheddar Cheese, Shredded**

Stir sour cream, mayonnaise and Ranch Dressing mix together, let set 5 minutes. While waiting, mix all other ingredients together, except cheese. Toss vegetable mixture with Ranch Dressing mix, top with grated cheese, chill, serve.

Delicious Chicken Salad

4-5	Cups Chicken, Cooked, Cut in Chunks
2	Tablespoons Salad Oil
2	Tablespoons orange Juice
1	Tablespoon Apple Cider Vinegar
1	Teaspoon Salt
3	Cups Cooked Rice
1½	Cups Seedless White Grapes
1½	Cups Celery, Sliced
1	Cup Pecans, Toasted and Chopped
1	Can Pineapple Tidbits, Drained (13½ ounces)
1	Can Mandarin oranges, Drained (11 ounces)
1½	Cups Mayonnaise

Mix oil, orange juice, vinegar and salt together. Stir into chicken, coating well. Set aside.

Toss cooked rice, fruits and nuts together, adding the mayonnaise last. Add chicken, stirring to blend well. Chill thoroughly before serving.

Loaded Pineapple Chicken Salad

3	Chicken Breasts, Deboned, Grilled and Seasoned With Lemon Pepper
1	Cup Raisins
½	Cup Walnuts, Chopped
½	Cup Blueberries
¼	Cup Carrots, Chopped
1	Can Pineapple Chunks (8 ounce), Drained (or Fresh Pineapple, chopped)
1	Can Mandarin oranges (8 ounce), Drained
¼-½	Cup Low Fat Mayonnaise, Yogurt, or Fruit Smoothie

Mix all ingredients listed above, moisten with your choice of mayonnaise, fruit smoothie, or yogurt. Very pretty served in a scooped out fresh pineapple. Vanilla or pineapple yogurt or smoothie would be good in this.

Pistachio Salad

1 **Container Of Whipped Topping**
   (8 ounce)
1 **Package Pistachio Instant Pudding**
   (3 ounce)
1 **Can Pineapple Tidbits** *(8 ounce),*
   Drained
1 **Cup Miniature Marshmallows**
½ **Cup Chopped Nuts,**
Pecans or Walnuts
Cherries to Garnish

Combine whipped topping and instant pudding, mix until pudding dissolves and mixture is smooth. Add pineapple, marshmallows, and nuts. Garnish with cherries and a few nuts.

Garden Pasta Salad

1	**Cup Cooked Ham, Cut in ½ inch cubes**
1	**Large Zucchini, Cut in ½ inch cubes**
1	**Medium Tomato, Diced**
½	**Medium Onion, Diced**
¼	**Cup Black Olives, Sliced**
8–10	**Fresh Mushrooms, Sliced**
1	**Tablespoon Capers**
2	**Tablespoons Olive Oil**
1	**Pound Pasta, Cooked and Drained**
½	**Cup Parmesan Cheese**
2	**Tablespoons Butter**

Sauté ham, zucchini, tomatoes, onion, mushrooms, olives, and capers in olive oil in a large skillet. Toss pasta (cooked according to package directions), with Parmesan cheese and butter. Add pasta to vegetable/ham mixture in skillet. Heat thoroughly. Serve warm.

Strawberry Salad

Topping:

2   **Cups Boiling Water**

1   **Large** (5.9 ounce) **Package Strawberry Jell-O or 2 Small Packages** (3 ounce)

1   **Package Frounceen Sliced Strawberries** (10 ounce)

Dissolve Jell-O in boiling water, add strawberries, refrigerate until soft set.

Crust:

½   **Cup Butter or Margarine, Melted**

¼   **Cup Brown Sugar**

2-3 **Cups Stick Pretzels**

Melt butter, add brown sugar, stir until mixed well. Break pretzels into halves, mix in butter mixture. Spread into a 9 x 13 inch glass baking dish. Bake at 350 degrees for 10 minutes, cool.

Filling:

1 **Cup Sugar**
1 **Package Cream Cheese** (8 ounce), **Softened**
1 **Container Whipped Topping** (12 ounce)

Cream sugar and cream cheese together, add whipped topping, stir until smooth. Spread this over cooled pretzel crust, top with soft set strawberry Jell-O. Refrigerate overnight.

Macaroni-Ham Salad

2-3	Cups Cooked Ham, Cubed
1	Pound Macaroni, Cooked and Drained
½	Cup Cheese, Grated
½	Cup Mayonnaise
⅓	Cup Pickle Relish, Sweet or Dill
¼	Cup Onion, Chopped
3	Eggs, Boiled, Chopped
2	Tablespoons Yellow Mustard
1	Teaspoon Salt
1	Teaspoon Black Pepper

Paprika to Garnish

Mix all ingredients listed above, in a large bowl, chill or serve warm.

Vegetable Salad

¾	**Cup Sugar**
¾	**Cup White or Apple Cider Vinegar**
½	**Cup Vegetable Oil**
1	**Teaspoon Salt and Pepper** (each)
1	**Can English Peas,** (15 ounce) **Drained**
1	**Can Shoepeg Corn,** (11 ounce) **Drained**
1	**Can French Cut Green Beans, Drained** (14½ ounce)
1	**Cup Celery, Chopped**
½	**Cup Bell Pepper, Chopped**
1	**Bunch Green Onions, Chopped**
1	**Jar Pimentos,** (2 ounce) **Drained**

Boil vinegar, sugar, oil, pepper and salt in a saucepan until sugar dissolves. Combine all the remaining ingredients in a medium bowl. Add vinegar mixture to vegetables, chill at least 12 hours. Can substitute fresh vegetables for the canned ones. Or can use broccoli, cauliflower or carrots for a variation.

Rice Salad

4   **Cups Cooked Brown Rice**
        (Follow Package Directions)
½   **Cup Bell Pepper, Chopped**
½   **Cup Red Onion, Chopped**
½   **Cup Carrots, Chopped**
½   **Cup Celery, Diced**
1   **Tomato, Chopped Chunky**
⅓   **Cup Olive Oil**
Salt and Pepper to Taste
Lemon Zest and Pecans, Optional

Mix cooked rice with all the vegetables. Mix a little olive oil, zest of a lemon, and salt And pepper together to form a dressing, pour over rice mixture. Toss, top with pecans, cover and refrigerate over night.

Special thanks to Rachel Day for sharing this recipe with me on a "Cooking With Hugh" show.

Waldorf Salad

2	Cups Red Apples, Diced and Unpeeled
1	Cup Celery, Sliced
½	Cup Mayonnaise
½	Cup Raisins
½	Cup Salted Peanuts
2	Tablespoons Lemon Juice

Pour lemon juice over apples. Add mayonnaise, raisins and celery, toss lightly. Chill until serving time, stir in or garnish with salted peanuts.

Bleu Cheese Dressing

4	Ounces Bleu Cheese, Crumbled
1	Cup Mayonnaise
1	Cup Sour Cream
1	Cup Buttermilk
1	Teaspoon Worcestershire Sauce
¼	Teaspoon Garlic Powder
¼	Teaspoon Salt

Mix all ingredients together with mixer or blender. Chill before serving. Store in the refrigerator up to two weeks.

Ranch Dressing

1	**Cup Buttermilk**
1	**Cup Mayonnaise**
1	**Tablespoon Dried Parsley**
1 ½	**Teaspoons Dried Onion Flakes**
¾	**Teaspoon Onion Salt**
¼	**Teaspoon Garlic Salt**

Mix all ingredients together. Chill, serve.

Thousand Island Dressing

1	Cup Mayonnaise
¼	Cup Barbeque or Chili Sauce
2	Tablespoons Onion, Finely Chopped
1	Teaspoon Worcestershire Sauce
1	Egg, Boiled and Finely Chopped
	Optional Ingredients:
2	Tablespoons Green Olives, Chopped
2	Tablespoons Sweet Peppers, Chopped (green or red)
1	Teaspoon Prepared Horseradish

Mix all ingredients together. Chill. Before serving, may need to stir in 1 or 2 tablespoons of milk for desired consistency.

Bar-B-Que Sauce

1   **Cup Spicy Brown Mustard**
½   **Cup Honey**
1-2   **Tablespoons Vinegar**
1   **Clove Garlic, Minced**
Celery Salt, to Taste
Pepper to Taste

Blend all ingredients together, pour or brush on cooked ribs, cook additional 10 to 15 minutes before serving.

Honey Mustard Sauce

1   **Cup Mayonnaise**
½   **Cup Honey**
½   **Cup Mustard**

Mix all together, great for dipping chicken fingers. A variation is to use half and half yellow mustard and brown mustard, adds a little spice. Also can decrease honey if too sweet for your taste. Very similar to honey mustard dipping sauces in many restaurants.

Sweet Garlic Butter Sauce

½ **Cup Butter**
½ **Teaspoon Garlic Salt**
½ **Cup Cane Syrup**

Melt butter, add garlic salt, bring to a slow boil, add syrup, bring back to slow boil, let simmer a few minutes, drizzle over biscuits, rolls, toast, etc.

White Sauce

Medium Consistency
- 1   **Tablespoon Butter**
- 1   **Tablespoon All-Purpose Flour**
- $1/8$ **Teaspoon Salt**
- **Dash Pepper**
- $3/4$ **Cup Milk**

Melt butter in a small sauce pan. Stir in flour, salt and pepper until evenly combined with no lumps. Stir in milk all at once. Cook and stir constantly over medium heat until thickened and smooth. Cook and stir one minute longer to completely cook flour.

For Thin White Sauce – use 1 cup milk.
For Thick White Sauce – use $1/2$ cup milk.

Glaze For Meats

1	**Cup White Corn Syrup**
1/3	**Cup Brown Sugar**
1/4	**Cup Brown Mustard**

Combine syrup, sugar and mustard, mixing well. Glaze meat last 20 minutes of cooking. This is a good glaze for a pork roast, a ham, or even turkey.

This is a favorite meat glaze of my Granny's.

Cranberry Glaze

1	Tablespoon Margarine
1/4	Cup Onion, Chopped
8	Ounces Whole Berry Cranberry Sauce
1/4	Cup Water
2	Tablespoons Brown Sugar
2	Tablespoons Chili Sauce
2	Tablespoons Soy Sauce
1	Tablespoon Lemon Juice
1	Teaspoon Yellow Mustard

Sauté onion in margarine until tender. Add remaining ingredients, cook, simmering 10 or 15 minutes. Use as a glaze on meat last 30 minutes of cooking, basting often.

Great on pork loin, can double the recipe, reserving half to serve as a warm side dish to serve over meat.

Maple Mustard Glaze

1	Teaspoon Butter
1/2	Cup Chicken Broth
1/4	Cup Pure Maple Syrup
2	Tablespoons Brown Spicy Mustard
1	Teaspoon Chopped Chives
1/2	Teaspoon Sage
1	Tablespoon Sour Cream

Melt butter over medium heat. Add broth, syrup, mustard, chives and sage. Bring to a boil and cook about 3 minutes. Stir in sour cream, reduce heat, simmer 3 to 5 minutes. Great served over pork chops or pork loin slices.

Broccoli Soup

1	**Small Bunch Broccoli, Chopped**
2	**Tablespoons Butter**
2	**Tablespoons Flour**
1	**Tablespoon Onion, Minced**
1	**Cup Milk**
Salt and Pepper	
2	**Cups Chicken Broth**
1	**Cup Sharp Cheddar Cheese, Grated**

Cook broccoli until tender (steam or in the microwave). Set aside.

Melt butter in a medium sauce pan. Stir in flour and onion until thoroughly combined. Stir in milk <u>all at once</u>. Cook and stir constantly over medium heat until thickened and smooth.

Put broccoli and butter flour mixture in a blender, blend until mixed thoroughly and broccoli chopped very fine. Pour back into medium sauce pan, add chicken broth, salt and pepper to taste, heat completely. Stir in cheese until melted. Serve warm.

Potato Cheese Soup

6   **Large Baking Potatoes**
2   **Chicken Bouillon Cubes**
2   **Cups Sour Cream**
½   **Cup Butter**
1   **Pound Velveeta Cheese**
6-10 **Slices of Bacon**

Brown bacon to a crisp. Peel and dice potatoes. Just barely cover potatoes with water, add bouillon cube, boil until potatoes are tender. Stir in butter, sour cream and Velveeta. When Velveeta is melted, soup is ready to serve, garnish with crumbled bacon.

Taco Stew

1 ½	**Pounds Ground Chuck**
½	**Pound Carroll's Pan Sausage** (Mild, Medium, or Hot)
1	**Onion, Chopped**
3	**Cans Diced Tomatoes with Chilies**
1	**Can Shoepeg Corn,** (undrained) (15 ¼ ounce)
1	**Can Chili Beans,** (undrained) (15 ½ ounce)
1	**Package Taco Seasoning** (1 ¼ ounce)
4	**Ounces Cheddar Cheese, Grated**

Brown meat and onion in a large pot or Dutch oven. Add all other ingredients except cheese. Mix well, cover and simmer on low heat 30 minutes to an hour. Top with grated cheese before serving. Serve with tortilla chips. Just as good or better next day.

(Taco Seasoning: 1 tablespoon Chili Powder, 2 teaspoons Onion Powder, 1 teaspoon each of Ground Cumin, Garlic Powder, Paprika, Oregano, and Sugar and ½ teaspoon Salt makes 3 tablespoons seasoning mix, which is equal to a ¼ ounce package of commercial seasoning.)

Oyster Stew

1   **Pint Oyster, Washed and Drained**
½   **Cup Butter**
1-2   **Quarts Whole Milk**
Salt and Pepper to Taste

Melt butter in a heavy pot. Add washed and drained oysters, salt and pepper to butter and cook until edges of oysters curl. Add milk. Heat thoroughly. Serve with saltine crackers.

Meats, Gravies
and
Main Dishes

Index

Favorite Recipes:

Title   Page Number

_____

_____

_____

_____

_____

_____

_____

_____

_____

_____

_____

_____

_____

_____

_____

_____

Beef Tenderloin

5-8   Pound Whole Beef Tenderloin
Horseradish Mustard
Pepper, Coarse Ground
Bacon
Onion, Sliced

Preheat oven to 375 degrees. Rub tenderloin with mustard, sprinkle with coarse ground black pepper. Wrap tenderloin with slices of bacon, place onion slices on top of bacon. Bake uncovered in oven from 1 to 2 hours, depending on desired doneness. Slice and serve. This is absolutely delicious, so tender, and should have meat from well done (ends of tenderloin) to rare.

Serve this with Parmesan Tomatoes, Simple and Easy Potatoes and the Layered Lettuce Salad… no restaurant can compare.

Carroll's Sausage

2-3 Links Carroll's Fresh Sausage
Mild, Medium or Hot, Pork or Beef, or Cheese

Cook on grill at medium heat in aluminum foil pan heavily sprayed with cooking spray, about 20 to 30 minutes, or until internal temperature reaches 175 to 180 degrees. Make sure edges of foil are turned up so dripping grease does not cause a flare-up. If using smoked sausage, grill on indirect heat about 10 to 15 minutes or until internal temperature reaches 175 to 180 degrees.

Bacon in Newpaper

6 or 8 Slices Bacon
Section of Newspaper (with no color pictures)
Two Sheets Paper Towels

Place one sheet of paper towel over half section of newspaper, place strips of bacon on paper towel, cover bacon with another paper towel, fold newspaper over paper towel covered bacon, cook in microwave on high for approximately 4 minutes. Remove bacon, discard paper towel, newspaper and grease. Easy cleanup!

Beef Brisket

6-10 Pound Beef Brisket
Salt and Pepper to Taste

Salt and pepper brisket heavily. Wrap as you would a beef roast, but turn the fat side up, and poke holes down into the brisket. As the brisket cooks, the fat will seep into the meat making it tasty and tender. Will need to cook at a much lower temperature than a roast beef, cook at 250 degrees for 6-8 hours or even lower — 180 degrees for 12-14 hours. If cooked properly, it is hard to beat the taste of a brisket.

Can also be cooked on smoker, but will need to be wrapped in foil after 2 or 3 hours and then cooked an additional 14 to 18 hours at 225 degrees.

(A brisket is a particular cut of beef, but it has more fat on the outside and inside than a regular beef roast. In our area, brisket is most often ground into hamburger, but very popular in the western part of the country as roast or Bar-b-que.)

Chipped Beef With Gravy

2   **Pounds Cooked Beef Roast, Sliced Very Thin**
4   **Tablespoons Butter, Melted**
2   **Tablespoons Flour**
1 ½   **Cups Milk**
Salt and Pepper to Taste

Combine melted butter and flour in a saucepan over low heat, stirring until starts to thicken. Add milk, season with salt and pepper. Bring to a slow boil, reducing heat to simmer, stirring continuously, until thickened. Place sliced roast in a baking dish, pour white gravy over roast, cover and bake in a 350 degree oven about 10 to 20 minutes. Serve over rice, creamed potatoes or toast. Can substitute some roast juices for part of milk, if desired.

Country Ham Slices

Center Cut Country Ham Slices
Vegetable Oil

Place small amount of vegetable oil in pan heated to medium high heat. Add slices of Ham. Cook turning often until slices are browned on both side. If desired use drippings for red eye gravy.

Red Eye Gravy

1 Cup Water or Coffee

After frying country ham, pour off part of fat, leaving scraps of ham and ham crusts and crumbs in skillet. Add water or coffee, and bring to a boil. Do not thicken, should be thin. Great served over grits, ham, or biscuits.

Grilled Hamburgers

1	**Pound Carroll's Pan Sausage** (Mild, Medium, or Hot)
2	**Pounds Ground Chuck**
1	**Green Bell Pepper, Chopped**
1/2	**Red Bell Pepper, Chopped**
1/2	**Onion, Chopped**
1/2	**Cup Ketchup**
3	**Tablespoons Steak Sauce**
1	**Teaspoon Garlic Salt**
1	**Teaspoon Celery Salt**
1	**Teaspoon Black Pepper**

Mix all ingredients together. Shape into patties, grill over medium heat (350 to 375 degrees) for 20 to 30 minutes until cooked to desired doneness. Turning when needed.

Double Battered Cubed Steak

4-6	**Pieces Cubed Pork or Beef Steak**
1 ½	**Cups Gravy Mix**
½	**Cup Buttermilk**
2-3	**Tablespoons Olive Oil**
½	**Cup Onions, Chopped**
½	**Cup Mushrooms, Sliced**
1	**Clove Garlic, Minced**
¼	**Cup Buttermilk**
1	**Can Diced Tomatoes** (14.5 ounce)
1	**Can Cream Of Mushroom Soup** (10 ¾ ounce)

Dredge cubed steak or pork in gravy mix, dip in ½ cup of buttermilk, dredge meat in gravy mix a second time. Brown meat on both sides in olive oil. Sauté chopped onions, mushrooms and garlic in pan with meat and oil. Mix ¼ cup of buttermilk, diced tomatoes and mushroom soup together. Pour soup mixture over meat and onions; simmer covered 20 to 30 minutes, turning meat occasionally.

Grilled Baby Back Ribs

1-2 Slabs Baby Back Ribs

Rub ribs with seasoning of your choice. Sear ribs on grill on both sides, wrap in foil, place back on grill, slow cook over low heat (about 300 degrees) for approximately three (3) hours. Baste with bar-b-que sauce, return to grill for additional 10 to 15 minutes.

Bar-B-Que Sauce

1   Cup Spicy Brown Mustard
½   Cup Honey
1-2   Tablespoons Vinegar
1   Clove Garlic, Minced
Celery Salt to Taste
Pepper to Taste

Blend all ingredients together, pour or brush on cooked ribs, cook additional 10 to 15 minutes before serving.

Ribs – Slow Grilled

Slab of Ribs
Seasoning
Foil

Rub ribs all over with seasoning. Sear both sides of ribs on grill at medium high heat. Wrap seared ribs in aluminum foil pouch, making sure edges of foil are turned up and sealed. Place back on grill, cook slowly at about 300 degrees for 3 hours or more.

Grilled Tenderloin Steaks

With Fruit Marinate

4   **Beef Tenderloins** (cut 1 to 1 ½ inch thick)
½   **Cup Orange Juice**
½   **Cup Pineapple Juice**
1   **Tablespoon Steak Sauce**
1   **Tablespoon Honey**
1   **Clove Garlic, Minced**
1   **Teaspoon Olive Oil**
½   **Teaspoon Salt**
Coarse Ground Black Pepper

Combine pineapple juice, orange juice, steak sauce, honey, garlic, olive oil, and salt. Pour over steaks in a shallow glass dish, turning to coat both sides. Cover and marinate in refrigerator about one hour. Pepper steaks, to taste, then grill, brushing with reserved marinate, over medium heat 7 to 10 minutes on each side until cooked to desired doneness. Discard remaining marinate.

Tenderloins AKA Filet Mignon.

Smothered Steak

1 ½   **Pound Boneless Round Steak**
1 ½   **Tablespoons Vegetable Oil**
2   **Large Onions, Sliced**
1   **Can Mushrooms** (6.5 ounce),
     Drained, Reserve Liquid
1   **Can Cream of Mushroom Soup**
     (10 ¾ ounce)
½   **Cup Water**
1 ½   **Teaspoons Garlic Salt**

Cut steak into thin strips. Brown steak in vegetable oil in a large heavy skillet on high heat. Add onions, sauté until tender. Mix soup, water, mushroom liquid and garlic salt. Pour over steak. Add mushrooms. Reduce heat, cover and simmer for one hour or until steak is tender.

Liver And Onions

4-8   Pieces Beef Liver (best cubed)
1   Onion, Sliced
Flour
Salt and Pepper to Taste
Cooking Oil

Sauté onions in small amount of oil in heavy skillet over medium heat. Remove onions from skillet. Add more oil, should have about ¼ inch oil in bottom of skillet, heat to medium high heat. Meanwhile season liver with salt and pepper, then dredge each piece of liver in flour, coating both sides. Place liver in hot oil, turn when bottom has browned lightly and red juices seep from top of liver. Cook 2 to 3 minutes more on each side, being careful not to overcook. Garnish with sautéed onions.

Baked Stew Beef and Potatoes

1 ½	Pounds Stew Beef, 1 inch Cubes
¼	Pound Bacon, Chopped
4-6	New Red Potatoes, Cubed
1	Teaspoon Salt
½	Teaspoon Pepper
½	Cup Bell Pepper, Diced Fine (Red, Yellow and Green)
½	Cup Onion, Diced Fine
½	Cup Fresh Mushrooms, Sliced
1	Can Cream of Mushroom Soup (10 ¾ ounce)
½	Cup Sour Cream
2	Cups Water
3	Cups Uncooked Minute Rice

Fry bacon pieces in a large skillet, brown stew beef in bacon drippings until browned on all sides. Add onions, potatoes, peppers and mushrooms to stew beef, sauté lightly. Add soup, sour cream and water to meat/vegetable mixture, cover and

_____

simmer for 20 minutes. Place uncooked Minute rice in bottom of a greased large baking dish, pour meat mixture over rice. Cover, bake at 350 degrees for about 1 hour.

Rolled Meat Loaf

½	**Pound Carroll's Pan Sausage** (Mild, Medium or Hot)
1 ½	**Pounds Ground Chuck**
2	**Eggs, Slightly Beaten**
2	**Cups Bread Crumbs**
1	**Can Tomato Sauce** (8 ounce)
1	**Teaspoon Basil**
1	**Teaspoon Salt and Pepper to Taste**
¾	**Cup Cheese, Shredded**
½	**Cup Bell Pepper, Diced Fine** (Red, Yellow and Green)
½	**Cup Onion, Diced Fine**
½	**Cup Fresh Mushrooms, Sliced**
¼	**Cup Black Olives, Sliced**

Combine beef, sausage, bread crumbs, eggs, tomato sauce, salt and pepper, mixing lightly, do not over mix. Place mixture on a piece of plastic wrap about 18 inches long and shape meat into a rectangle about ¾ to 1 inch thick. Sprinkle cheese, peppers, onion, olives and mushrooms evenly over meat rectangle. Lifting one edge of plastic wrap, roll meat jelly roll style, sealing in

---

all the vegetables. Place in a large foil lined baking pan with seam side of meat down and remove plastic wrap. Bake at 350 degrees for about one hour. Let set a few minutes before serving. This almost taste like pizza, but without the crust.

Meatballs –
Bacon Wrapped

1 **Pound Carroll's Pan Sausage**
(Mild, Medium or Hot)
2 **Pounds Ground Chuck**
½ **Teaspoon Italian Seasoning**
Bacon Slices, Cut in Half

Mix ground chuck, sausage and seasoning mix. Form meatballs to desired size. Wrap each meatball in ½ slice of bacon. Place meatballs in foil lined 9 x 13 inch baking pan. Cover with foil and bake at 350 degrees for 30 to 40 minutes. Add cooked meatball to tomato mixture, recipe next page:

Tomato Sauce:

½	**Cup Bell Pepper** (or Jalapeno)
½	**Cup Onions, Chopped**
¼	**Cup Olive Oil**
1	**Clove Garlic, Minced**
2	**Tablespoons Butter**
½	**Teaspoon Italian Seasoning**
2	**Ounce Cans Tomato Sauce** (15 ounce)
2	**Tablespoons Honey**
2	**Tablespoons Brown Sugar**

Sauté garlic, bell pepper, onions in butter and olive oil in large pan. Add seasoning. Mix tomato sauce, sugar and honey together, add to sautéed mixture. Add cooked meatball to tomato mixture and simmer covered for 20 minutes.

Meat Loaf

¼	**Pound Carroll's Pan Sausage** (Mild, Medium or Hot)
1½	**Pound Ground Chuck**
1	**Egg, Slightly Beaten**
1	**Cup Bread Crumbs**
¾	**Cup Ketchup**
2	**Tablespoons Worcestershire Sauce**
1	**Teaspoon Salt and Pepper to Taste**
2	**Tablespoons Brown Sugar**

Combine beef, sausage, bread crumbs, egg, Worcestershire sauce and ½ cup ketchup, salt and pepper, mixing lightly, do not over mix. Shape into a loaf, place on a foil lined baking pan. Bake at 350 degrees for 45 minutes. Mix ¼ cup ketchup and brown sugar together, pour over meat loaf, cook additional 10 to 15 minutes.

30 Minute Supper

1¼	**Pounds Ground Chuck**
¼	**Pound Carroll's Pan Sausage** (Mild, Medium or Hot)
1	**Onion, Chopped**
1	**Can Tomato Soup, Undiluted** (10 ½ ounce)
1	**Small Cabbage, Chopped**

Brown meat and onion in a large skillet or Dutch oven over medium high heat. Add soup and stir until heated thoroughly. Add chopped cabbage. Salt to taste. Reduce heat to medium low, cook, stirring occasionally, until cabbage is desired tenderness. Serve with cornbread.

Oven Baked Pot Roast

4-5 Pound Beef Roast
1   Envelope Onion Soup Mix
1   Cup Water
2   Tablespoons Worcestershire Sauce
Salt and Pepper to Taste

Place roast in a foil lined roasting pan, salt and pepper roast to taste. Sprinkle soup mix over roast. Mix water and Worcestershire sauce, pour in roast pan. Cover roast with foil, securely, bake in a preheated 350 degree oven for 2 or 3 hours.

Pot Roast With Vegetables

4-5   Pound Rump Roast
4   Small Potatoes, Peeled and Cut In Half
2   Carrots, Peeled and Cut Into 2 inch Slices
2   Stalks Celery, Cut into 2 inch Pieces
2   Medium Onions, Sliced
2   Cups Water
Salt and Pepper to Taste

Place pot roast in a foil lined roasting pan. Add vegetables to pan, placing around pot roast. Sprinkle pot roast and vegetables with salt and pepper, add water to pan. Cover with foil and bake in a 350 degree oven for about 1 ½ to 2 hours.

Bone-In Prime Rib Roast

4	Pound Bone-In Prime Rib Roast
4-5	Garlic Cloves
¾	Cup Dales Steak Sauce
¼	Cup Worcestershire Sauce
½	Teaspoon Seasoning Salt
½	Teaspoon Celery Salt

Marinade

½	Cup Honey
½	Cup Spicy Brown Mustard

Trim around end of rib bones of roast. From top of roast, cut holes in roast by inserting a large knife in the roast to within 1 inch of bottom of roast. Insert a whole garlic clove into each hole. Combine Dales, Worcestershire, and salts in small bowl. Using a meat injector, finish filling the holes with sauce. Place roast in large baking dish and pour remaining sauce over roast. Refrigerate at least 4 to 5 hours or overnight. Bake at 300 degrees for 2 ½ to 3 hours. Garnish with pineapple slices and/or cherries and pour marinade over before serving.

Skillet Sausage with Peppers and Onions

1	**Link Carroll's Fresh Link Sausage** (Mild, Medium, or Hot)
2	**Bell Peppers, Roughly Chopped**
½	**Onion, Roughly Chopped**
½	**Pound Mushrooms, Roughly Chopped**
¼	**Cup Olive Oil**

Heat olive oil in large cast-iron skillet over medium heat. Add peppers, onions, mushrooms, and sausage. Cover and let cook for at least 30 to 45 minutes until sausage is thoroughly cooked (internal temperature of at least 160 degrees)

Tater Tot Casserole

2	**Pounds Ground Chuck**
1	**Can Cream of Celery Soup** *(10 ¾ ounce)*
1	**Can Cream of Chicken Soup** *(10 ¾ ounce)*
2	**Cups Sour Cream**
3	**Cups Cheese, Shredded**
1	**Bag Frozen Tater Tots** *(24-32 ounce)*

Brown ground chuck — salt and pepper to taste, drain. Spread browned chuck in bottom of a 9 X 13 inch greased baking pan. Mix soups and sour cream together, pour over meat layer. Spread shredded cheese over soup/sour cream mixture. Cover cheese with tater tots. Bake at 350 degrees for about 40 minutes until browned and bubbly.

Beef Shish-Ka-Bobs

1 inch Thick Sirloin Steak
Red and Green Bell Pepper,
Seeded and Cut In 1 ½ inch Pieces
Onions, Cut In 1 ½ inch Pieces
Sliced Bacon, Cut Into 1 ½ inch Pieces
Salt, Pepper, Garlic Salt, and
Celery Salt to Taste

Trim all fat from steak, cut steak into 1 ½ inch pieces. Thread on skewer in this order: 2 pieces of steak, onion, bacon, bell pepper, then followed by 2 pieces of steak. Repeat, keeping piece of bacon between onion and pepper and ending with 2 pieces of steak. Season to taste. Place on grill, searing both sides, then grill on medium heat about 15 minutes, turning when needed. Remove from heat, seal in aluminum foil, place back on grill, cook about 5 to 10 minutes, until desired doneness.

Chili

½	**Pound Carroll's Pan Sausage** (Mild, Medium or Hot)
1	**Pound Lean Ground Chuck**
1	**Cup Onion, Chopped**
1	**Cup Bell Pepper**
3	**Cloves Garlic, Minced**
¼	**Cup Olive Oil**
2	**Tablespoons Butter**
½	**Cup Smoked Ham Hocks** (optional)
1	**Can Diced Tomatoes** (14.5 ounce)
1	**Can Tomato Sauce** (8 ounce)
1	**Small Can Chili Beans** (16 ounce)
¼	**Cup Barbeque Sauce**
1	**Tablespoon Barbeque Seasoning**
2	**Teaspoons Chili Powder**
1	**Teaspoon Basil Leaf, Chopped**

Salt and Pepper to Taste

CHILI (continued)

Sauté bell pepper, onion, and garlic in butter and olive oil until tender. Combine ground chuck and sausage and add to onions and peppers. Add ham hocks. Brown meat with onion and peppers over medium high heat. In mixing bowl, mix tomatoes and tomato sauce, beans, chili powder, barbeque sauce and seasoning, basil, salt, and pepper. Add to skillet with browned meat. Simmer over low heat 45 minutes to an hour. Great served with grated cheese and sour cream on the side.

Beef Burrito

1   **Pound Carroll's Link Beef Smoked Sausage, Sliced**
¾   **Cup Onions**
¾   **Cup Mushrooms, Sliced**
½   **Cup Butter**
1   **Tomato, Chopped**
Flour Tortillas

Sauté onions, mushrooms and sausage in butter until sausage reaches 165 degrees and onions are tender. Place sausage and onion mixture in middle of tortilla, top with chopped tomatoes, roll tortilla. May add cheese, salsa and/or sour cream, to taste.

Ground Beef Casserole

¼	**Pound Carroll's Pan Sausage** (Mild, Medium, or Hot)
1	**Pound Ground Beef**
1	**Large Onion, Sliced**
1	**½ Cup Cheddar Cheese, Shredded**
1	**Large Potato, Sliced Very Thin**
2	**Cans Cream Of Mushroom Soup** (10 ¾ ounce)

Lightly brown ground beef and sausage. Layer meat in a greased baking dish, top with Sliced onions and shredded cheese. Completely cover cheese with potatoes sliced very thin. Pour soup over potatoes. Cover with foil and bake at 400 degrees for 30 minutes, uncover, cook about 10 to 15 minutes longer. To garnish, sprinkle cheese over top before serving.

Hamburger Twist

Meat Filling:

1/4	**Pound Carroll's Pan Sausage** (Mild, Medium, or Hot)
1	**Pound Ground Beef**
1/2	**Cup Celery, Chopped**
1/2	**Cup Green Peppers, Chopped**
1/2	**Cup Onion, Chopped**
1/4	**Cup Cream of Mushroom Soup**
1	**Cup Cheese, Shredded**

Brown meat, add celery, peppers, onions, sauté. Mix in 1/4 cup cream of mushroom soup. Spoon meat mixture down middle of dough rectangle that has been placed on cookie sheet. Sprinkle with one cup of cheese. Fold 1 inch cut strips of dough over meat filling. Bake 15 to 20 minutes in a preheated 425 degree oven.

Crust:

2	**Cups Biscuit Mix**
1/2	**Cup Cold Water**

Mix biscuit mix and cold water until soft dough forms. Beat vigorously about 15 to 20 strokes, roll dough out on flour covered waxed paper into a 14 x 12 inch rectangle. Place on a greased, foil lined baking sheet. Make cuts 2 to 3 inches long at 1 inch intervals on sides of dough. Fold strips over meat filling. Can substitute frozen biscuits that have been thawed and rolled together to form rectangle. To create glossy shine, can mix one egg with one tablespoon water and brush over dough before cooking. For sauce, 1 can cream of mushroom soup (10 ¾ ounce) — less ¼ cup used in meat.

Sauce:
- ½ **Cup Cheese, Shredded**
- ¼ **Cup Milk**

Mix remaining soup with milk and cheese, heat in microwave until hot and cheese has melted. Serve as sauce or gravy over meat twist.

Baked Spaghetti

½	**Pound Carroll's Pan Sausage**
	(Mild, Medium, Or Hot)
1	**Pound Ground Chuck**
½	**Onion, Chopped**
1	**Green and Red Bell Pepper, Chopped**
1	**Teaspoon Garlic Powder**
	(or 2 cloves garlic, minced)
2	**Teaspoons Italian Seasoning**
1	**Teaspoon Black Pepper**

Salt to Taste

1	**Jar Spaghetti Sauce** (32 ounce)
½	**Box Angel Hair Pasta**

Parmesan Cheese, Grated
Mozzarella Cheese, Grated

Brown ground chuck and sausage. Sauté onions, pepper, and garlic along with meat. Mix seasonings with meat mixture.

BAKED SPAGHETTI (continued)

Add spaghetti sauce. Simmer about 20 to 30 minutes. In the meantime, prepare pasta according to package directions. Drain pasta, add spaghetti sauce mixture to pasta, mixing well. Layer half of spaghetti mixture in a greased 9 x 13 inch baking dish, cover spaghetti with mozzarella cheese, pour remaining spaghetti mixture over cheese. Bake approximately 20 to 25 minutes, top with parmesan and grated mozzarella and/ or cheddar cheese, if desired, let set 10 minutes. Serve.

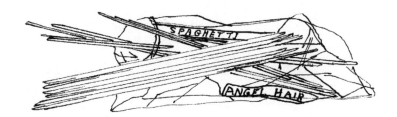

Beef Stroganoff

3	**Pounds Ground Chuck**
1	**Onion, Chopped**
¼	**Cup Butter**
1	**Can Sliced Mushrooms** (6.5 ounce)
1	**Can Cream Of Mushroom Soup** (10 ¾ ounce)
1	**Cup Sour Cream**

Salt and Pepper to Taste

Sauté ground chuck and onion in butter until onions are tender and beef has browned. Add mushrooms with liquid, soup and sour cream. Season with salt and pepper to taste. Reduce heat, cover and simmer for 20 to 30 minutes, stirring occasionally. Serve over rice or noodles.

Quick and Easy Beef Casserole

1	**Pound Ground Chuck**
1	**Package Hash Brown Potatoes** (24 ounce), **Thawed**
1	**Can Cream of Mushroom Soup** (10 ¾ ounce)
1	**Cup Sour Cream**
2	**Cups Cheese, Shredded**
1	**Onion, Chopped**
2	**Cans French-Fried Onions** (2.8 ounce)

In a large skillet, brown ground chuck that has been salted and peppered to taste. Drain. Add thawed hash brown potatoes to browned chuck, soup, sour cream, cheese and onion; mix well. Pour mixture into a large greased baking dish, bake in a 350 degree preheated oven for 30 minutes. Remove from oven, top with French-Fried onions then bake an additional 15 minutes.

Beef Macaroni and Cheese Casserole

2	Pounds Ground Chuck
1	Pound Box Elbow Macaroni
2	Cups Onion, Chopped
2	Cups Green Bell Pepper, Chopped
2	Cloves Garlic, Chopped
3	Cups Crushed Tomatoes (fresh or canned)
2	Tablespoons Vegetable Oil
1	Teaspoon Basil, Oregano, and Cumin
2	Cups Grated Cheese

Salt and Pepper to Taste

Cook macaroni according to package directions. Drain and set aside. Sauté pepper, onion and garlic in oil until soft in large skillet. Brown ground beef with peppers and onions. Add tomatoes, salt, pepper, spices and cooked macaroni to ground beef mixture. Mix well, pour into a greased 9 X 13 inch baking dish. Bake in a 350 degree oven for 15-20 minutes, top with cheese, cook additional 5-10 minutes until cheese is melted.

Ham–Broccoli Casserole

1	**Package Frozen Broccoli** *(16 ounce)*, **Cooked**
1½	**Cup Cheese, Shredded**
1	**Cup Cooked Ham, Chopped**
1	**Cup Mayonnaise**
1	**Can Cream of Mushroom Soup** *(10 ¾ ounce)*
2	**Eggs**

Combine all ingredients, pour into a greased baking dish, cook at 350 degrees for about 30 minutes, until quiche like consistency.

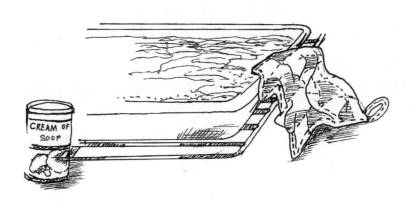

Sausage Grits

½-1	**Pound Carroll's Pan Sausage,** (Mild, Medium or Hot)
1	**Cup Water**
1	**Cup Chicken Stock**
1	**Cup Quick Grits**
½	**Teaspoon Salt**
1	**Cup Heavy Cream**
¼	**Cup Butter**
¼	**Teaspoon Garlic Powder**
½	**Cup Parmesan Cheese, Grated**

Cook sausage, scrambling well – set aside. Bring water and chicken stock to a boil in a two quart pot, stir in grits and salt. Reduce heat, cover and cook about 5 minutes, stirring occasionally. Stir in butter, heavy cream and garlic powder. When butter has melted stir in sausage and Parmesan cheese. Serve.

(May need to add more water to achieve desired consistency.)

Sausage/Macaroni Casserole

1	**Pound Carroll's Pan Sausage,** (Mild, Medium Or Hot)
1	**Medium Onion, Chopped**
½	**Green Pepper, Chopped**
2	**Tablespoons Flour**
½	**Teaspoon Salt**
1½	**Cups Milk**
8	**Ounce Cheddar Cheese, Shredded**
8	**Ounce Package Macaroni** (cooked)

Cook macaroni according to package directions, drain and set aside. Cook sausage, onion and pepper in frying pan over medium heat until sausage has browned. Drain sausage, add flour and salt to sausage mixture, blending well. Gradually add milk; cook over low heat, stirring constantly, until thickened. Stir in drained macaroni and half the cheese. Spoon mixture into a lightly greased baking dish, sprinkle with remaining cheese. Bake uncovered for 30 minutes at 400 degrees.

Sausage and Rice

1	**Pound Carroll's Pan Sausage** (Mild, Medium or Hot)
¼	**Cup Onion, Finely Diced**
¼	**Cup Celery, Finely Diced**
½	**Green Bell Pepper, Finely Diced**
1	**Teaspoon Seasoning Salt**
1	**Package Long-Grain Wild Rice With Seasoning** (5 ounce)
1 ½	**Cups Chicken Broth**

Brown sausage in a large skillet over medium-high heat. Add onion, celery, bell pepper, cook until soft, about 3 to 5 minutes. Add seasoning salt, rice, and chicken broth. Stir to combine. Reduce heat and cook, covered for 20 to 25 minutes, or until rice has absorbed all moisture. Fluff with fork and serve.

Sausage and Rice Casserole

1   **Pound Carroll's Pan Sausage,**
    (Mild, Medium or Hot)
2   **Onions, Chopped**
2   **Cans Cream of Mushroom Soup**
    (10 ¾ ounce)
1   **Can Cream of Chicken Soup**
    (10 ¾ ounce)
1   **Can Sliced Mushrooms** (6.5 ounce)
1   **Cup Water**
1   **Box Wild Rice Mix, Cooked**
    According to Directions

Brown sausage and onions together. Drain any grease, add cooked rice and mix well. Add soups, mushrooms and water to sausage rice mixture, pour into a greased 9 x 13 inch baking dish. Bake at 350 degrees for 30 to 40 minutes.

Sausage Stuffed Tomatoes

½-1   **Pound Carroll's Pan Sausage,**
      (Mild, Medium or Hot)
½-1   **Pound Lean Ground Chuck**
½   **Bell Pepper, Chopped**
½   **Onion, Chopped**
1   **Jalapeno Pepper, Chopped**
2-4   **Tablespoons Olive Oil**
      Season to Taste With: Pepper,
      Garlic and Celery Salt, and
      Nature's Seasoning
4-6   **Firm Ripe Tomatoes**
Grated Cheddar Cheese

Mix all ingredients (adding olive oil makes mixing easier), except tomatoes and cheese. Cut off top ¼ tomato; scoop out inside of tomato (reserve for salsa, soup, etc.). Stuff tomatoes with meat mixture; bake stuffed tomatoes at 350 degrees for one hour. After baking, sprinkle with cheddar cheese. Serve.

Sausage and Tomato Sandwiches

1   **Pound Carroll's Smoked Link Sausage,** (Mild, Medium or Hot)
2   **Ripe Tomatoes**
Sandwich Bread
Mayonnaise
Salt and Pepper to Taste

Peel skin (casing) from smoked sausage, slice length wise, cook sausage in oven, microwave or pan fry until internal temperature reaches 165 degrees. Cut sausage into bread length pieces, layer sliced tomato and sausage on mayonnaised bread. Salt and pepper tomato to taste. Top with second slice of mayonnaised bread. Enjoy.

Baked Dijon Chops

4   **Boneless Pork Chops**
2   **Tablespoons Dijon Mustard**
1   **Tablespoon Vegetable Oil**
4   **Tablespoons Bread Crumbs**
2   **Tablespoons Parmesan Cheese**
1   **Teaspoon Parsley**
Salt and Pepper to Taste

Mix mustard and oil together, spread on both sides of pork chop. Mix bread crumbs, Parmesan cheese, parsley, salt and pepper together. Dredge each chop in bread crumb mixture. Place in a foil lined pan, bake 20 to 30 minutes, turning chops once, until internal temperature reaches at least 165 degrees and chops are nicely browned.

Hawaiian Pork Chops

6	**Boneless Pork Chops, ½ inch Thick**
1	**Can Pineapple Slices (20 ounce), Drained, Reserve Juice**
2	**Tablespoons Honey**
1	**Tablespoon Brown Sugar**

Salt and Pepper to Taste

Place pork chops seasoned with salt and pepper in a greased baking dish. Mix 1/3 cup of the pineapple juice with the honey and brown sugar. Pour half the juice mixture over the chops, place the pineapple slices on each chop, pour remaining juice mixture over pineapple. Cover with foil and bake in a 350 degree oven for 30 minutes. Remove foil, bake another 15 to 20 minutes or until chops are done.

Fried Pork Chops

6-8   Bone-In or Boneless Pork Chops
1-1½ Cups Self-Rising Flour
Cooking Oil
Salt and Pepper to Taste

Combine flour, salt and pepper. Dredge pork chops in flour, covering both sides. Heat about ½ inch cooking oil in a heavy skillet to medium heat. Place chops in hot oil. Cook until golden brown on bottom and red juices are seeping from top of chops. Turn, cook 7 to 10 minutes more or until chops are done. (may need to add more oil to prevent chops from sticking to pan before turning.) Internal temperature of chops should be at least 165 degrees.

Gravy:
¼-½ Cup Water
3-4   Tablespoons Flour

After cooking chops, remove from pan. Add water and flour to drippings in pan (if too much oil in pan, pour some off, leaving 2 or 3 tablespoons oil in pan). Cook over medium heat, stirring constantly to loosen pork chop crumbs and to bring to gravy consistency (may need to add more water or flour to get right consistency). Reduce heat, cover and simmer for 10 minutes or so. Can place chops back in skillet with gravy while simmering or serve gravy on the side.

Pork Chops On Rice

6-8   **Pork Chops, ½ inch Thick Seasoned with Salt and Pepper to Taste**

2   **½ Cups Uncooked Minute Rice**

2   **½ Cups Water**

1   **Cup Orange Juice**

1   **Can Cream of Chicken Soup**
        (10 ¾ ounce)

Season pork chops with salt and pepper then brown on both sides in skillet. Place uncooked minute rice in large baking dish sprayed with cooking spray. Pour water and juice over rice. Arrange pork chops on rice, pour chicken soup over chops. Cover and bake at 350 degrees for 45 minutes. Uncover and bake for additional 10 minutes.

Stuffed Chops

4	Carroll's Bacon Wrapped Sausage Stuffed Pork Chops
1/2	Onion, Chopped
1/2	Bell Pepper, Chopped
1/4	Cup Olive Oil
2	Tablespoons Butter
1	Can Cream of Celery Soup (10 3/4 ounce)
1	Soup Can Water
1/2	Teaspoon Celery Salt and Garlic Salt

Salt and Pepper to Taste

Bake stuffed pork chops uncovered at 350 degrees for 30 minutes in a 9 x 13 inch foil lined pan. Sauté onions and bell pepper in olive oil and butter. Mix water, soup, salts, and pepper, heat in microwave for 3 to 5 minutes, stirring every minute or so. Add sautéed onions and bell peppers to soup mixture, pour over pork chops, cover with foil, return to oven and bake an additional 30 minutes. Let stand 10 minutes, covered. Serve.

Smoked Pork Chops – Salsa Style

4	Smoked Pork Chops (¾ inch thick)
1	Jalapeno Pepper, Sliced
1	Large Onion, Chopped
¾	Cup Bell Pepper, Chopped
¼	Cup Olive Oil
¼	Cup Cilantro, Chopped
4-5	Tomatoes, Diced
	Season to taste with: Salt, Pepper, Garlic Salt, Celery Salt, and Nature's Seasoning

Preheat pan with olive oil, sauté peppers, onion, and cilantro about 8 to 10 minutes, add diced tomatoes and seasoning to desired taste. Simmer another 5 to 6 minutes. Place the smoked pork chops in pan with salsa, cover and cook about 10 minutes, turning chops after 5 minutes. Serve chops smothered with salsa. (can use store bought salsa instead of homemade, but be sure to heat salsa thoroughly before adding chops.)

Baked Stuffed Pork Chops

3   **Carroll's Bacon Wrapped Sausage Stuffed Pork Chops**
1   **Can Cream of Mushroom Soup**
      (10 ¾ ounce)
½   **Soup Can of Water**
Garlic Salt and Celery Salt to Taste
Pepper to Taste

Cut each stuffed chop into four slices, creating four medallion shaped pieces. Season with salts and pepper to taste. Place each piece in a foil lined baking pan. Mix soup and water, pour over chops, cover with foil, bake in a preheated 350 degree oven about 30 minutes. Remove foil and bake an additional 15 minutes.

Stuffed Pork Loin

½	**Pound Carroll's Pan Sausage**
	(Mild, Medium or Hot)
4-5	**Pound Boneless Pork Loin**
	Butterfly Cut
½	**Pound Lean Ground Chuck**
1	**Cup Stuffing Mix**
¼	**Cup Olive Oil**
½	**Onion, Coarsely Chopped**
1	**Bell Pepper, Sliced**

Smoked Bacon, Sliced

Season to Taste with: Pepper, Garlic and Celery Salt, and Nature's Seasoning

Mix all ingredients (adding olive oil makes mixing easier), except bacon, onion and bell pepper. Butterfly cut pork loin, stuff loin with meat/ stuffing mixture.

_____

Place bell pepper slices and onion on stuffing in-side pork loin, wrap loin with bacon. Place in a foil lined pan and bake in a preheated 350 degree oven for approximately 90 minutes, uncovered for first 45 minutes, then cover with foil, until inter-nal temperature of pork loin reaches 165 degrees. Let stand 10 minutes, slice and serve.

Honey Glazed Sesame Pork Tenderloin

2-4   **Pound Pork Tenderloin**
¾   **Cup Soy Sauce**
¼   **Cup Worcestershire Sauce**
1   **Clove Garlic, Minced**
2   **Tablespoons Olive Oil**
½   **Cup Honey**
¼   **Cup Brown Sugar**
Sesame Seeds, Optional

Mix soy sauce, Worcestershire sauce, garlic and olive oil together. Marinate tenderloin in glass dish 2 hours at room temperature or in refrigerator overnight.

Mix honey and brown sugar together. Remove tenderloin from marinade and roll in honey sugar mixture, coating well. Sprinkle with sesame seeds if desired, cover with foil and bake at 375 degrees until internal temperature reaches 160 degrees. Let set 5 minutes, slice and serve.

Pork Roast – Oven Baked

3-5 Pound Boston Butt Pork Roast
1 Cup Water
Salt and Pepper to Taste

Place pork roast in a foil lined baking pan, fat side down, season with salt and pepper. Pour water into bottom of pan, cover with foil and bake in a 375 degree oven for 1 ½ to 2 ½ hours or until center of roast reaches 165 degrees.

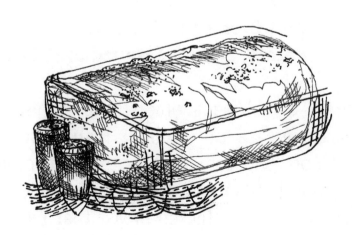

Brunswick Stew

½	Vidalia Onion, Chopped
2	Tablespoons Bacon Grease
2	Pound Pulled Pork
1	Can Diced Tomatoes (14.5 ounce)
1	Pound Ground Chuck, Browned
1	Boneless, Skinless Chicken Breast, Cooked and Chopped
1 ½	Cup Chicken Broth
2	Cups Ketchup
½	Cup BBQ Sauce
2	Tablespoons Brown Sugar
2	Tablespoons Worcestershire Sauce
1	Teaspoon Hot Sauce
1	Small Can Early Young Peas (8 ounce)
1	Can Creamed Corn (14 ¾ ounce)
1	Potato, Baked, Skinned and Cubed

Sauté ½ of a Vidalia onion in 2 tablespoons of bacon grease on medium high heat. Add pulled pork and tomatoes, to sautéed onions. Add ground chuck that has been browned and boneless, skinless chicken breast that has been cooked and chopped. Pour chicken broth in pot

———————————

with meat and tomatoes, continuing to cook on medium high heat. To meat/tomato mixture, stir in ketchup, BBQ sauce, brown sugar, Worcestershire sauce and hot sauce. Next add peas, corn, and potato. Add salt and pepper to taste, lower heat and simmer for at least one hour. (Easy way to bake potato: wrap potato in a paper towel and microwave for 6 minutes.)

Special thanks to Dr. Morris Leis for sharing this recipe with me on a "Cooking With Hugh" show.

Oxtails Over Rice

1 ½   **Pound Oxtail, Trimmed, Leaving Little Fat**
1   **Onion**
1   **Bell Pepper**
Frozen Vegetable Stew Mix
      (onions, carrots, celery, potatoes)
Seasoning to Taste: Salt, Garlic Salt, Greek Seasoning, Pepper
Rice (cooked according to package directions)

Season trimmed and washed oxtails with garlic salt, Greek seasoning, pepper, etc., place In boiling water along with chunks of onion and bell pepper (with seeds removed). Bring back to a boil, cover and simmer for about 1 hour, add vegetable stew mix, simmer another 30 minutes or until both meat and vegetables are tender. Spoon oxtail stew over cooked rice — ready to serve. Can also be cooked in a crock pot.

Thanks Valerie McKeller for this recipe.

Personal Pizza

¼	**Pound Carroll's Pan Sausage**
	(Mild, Medium or Hot)
½	**Pound Ground Beef**
8	**Frozen Biscuits, Thawed**
I	**Can Tomato Sauce** (8 ounce)

Mozzarella Cheese
Parmesan Cheese

Brown ground beef and sausage. Flatten biscuits with hand or rolling pin. Spread meat on flattened biscuits, pour tomato sauce over each. Sprinkle with cheeses and bake in 400 degree oven until biscuits are brown, about 10 to 15 minutes.

Chicken Pizza

1/4	**Cup Oil**
1	**Tablespoon Coarse Ground Corn Meal**
1	**Package Crescent Dinner Rolls** (8 Roll Package)
2	**Whole Skinless Chicken Breasts, Cooked and Deboned**
1	**Can Sliced Mushrooms** (6.5 ounce), **Drained**
1	**Large Onion, Sliced**
1	**Large Green Pepper, Sliced**
1	**Can Spaghetti or Pizza Sauce** (16 ounce)
2	**Cups Mozzarella Cheese, Shredded**
1/4	**Cup Parmesan Cheese**
1/4	**Teaspoon Oregano**

Oil pizza pan, sprinkle corn meal over oil. Press dinner rolls together in pan, forming one solid crust. Cut cooked chicken into one inch cubes. Sauté onions, pepper and mushroom, add chicken, heat thoroughly.

Spread spaghetti sauce over uncooked dinner roll crust, top with chicken mixture. Sprinkle with oregano and parmesan cheese. Top with mozzarella. Bake at 425 degrees for 20 minutes, until crust is done.

Chicken Divan

2	Packages Frozen Broccoli (10 ounce), Cooked
2	Cups Chicken or Turkey, Cooked and Chopped
2	Cans Cream of Chicken Soup (10 ¾ ounce)
½	Cup Mayonnaise
½	Tablespoon Lemon Juice
½	Teaspoon Curry Powder
½	Cup Cheddar Cheese, Grated
½	Cup Bread Crumbs
1	Tablespoon Butter

Cook frozen broccoli about 6 to 8 minutes in microwave on high, stirring every 2 minutes. Place cooked broccoli in microwave safe baking dish. Layer cooked and chopped chicken or turkey over broccoli. Combine cream of chicken soup, mayonnaise, lemon juice and curry powder. Spread over chicken. Mix cheese, butter and bread crumbs together, sprinkle over mayonnaise mixture. Cook in microwave on high for 12 minutes, turning dish quarter turn every 3 to 4 minutes.

Chicken Noodle Cheese Casserole

16	**Ounce Bag Egg Noodles**
3	**Cans White Meat Flaked Chicken** (16 ounce)
1	**Can Cream Of Chicken Soup** (10 ¾ ounce)
1	**Can Cream Of Celery Soup** (10 ¾ ounce)
2	**Cups Sour Cream**
3	**Cups Cheese, Shredded**
1	**Sleeve Ritz Crackers**
1	**Stick Butter, Melted**

Cook noodles according to package directions. Drain juice from canned chicken, mix chicken, cheese, soups and sour cream together well. Pour into a 9x13 inch greased baking dish, top with crumbled Ritz crackers. Drizzle melted butter over crackers and cook at 350 degrees for 40-45 minutes.

Chicken and Rice Casserole

4	**Chicken Breast Halves, Skinless and Boneless**
¾	**Cup Uncooked Long-Grain Rice**
⅓	**Cup Water**
1	**Can Cream of Chicken Soup** (10 ¾ ounce)
2	**Cups Mixed Vegetables** (Peas, Corn, Carrots, Broccoli, etc.)
1	**Teaspoon Celery Salt**
1	**Teaspoon Onion Salt**
½	**Cup Cheese, Grated**

Lightly brown the chicken breast halves. Stir rice, water, soup, vegetables, and salts together. Pour this mixture into a shallow baking dish. Top with lightly browned chicken, cover and bake at 375 degrees for 45 minutes or until done. Remove from oven and top with grated cheese.

30 Minute Chicken and Rice

4	Cups Chicken, Cooked and Cubed
6	Ounce Package Wild Rice Mix
	(Cooked according to package directions)
1	Can French Cut Green Beans
	(15 ounce)
½	Cup Sliced Water Chestnuts
1	Cup Slivered Almonds
	(Reserve ¼ cup for garnish)
1	Can Cream Celery Soup (10 ¾ ounce)
1	Cup Mayonnaise
1	Onion, Finely Chopped

Salt and Pepper to Taste

Mix cubed, cooked chicken and cooked wild rice together. Stir in green beans, water chestnuts and almonds. Mix soup, mayonnaise, onion, salt and pepper together, gently stir into chicken mixture. Top with reserved almonds, bake at 350 degrees in a 9 x 13 inch baking dish.

Chicken Pot Pie

4	**Cups Cooked Chicken, Chopped**
3	**Eggs, Boiled**
2	**Cups Chicken Broth**
1	**Can Cream Of Celery Soup** (10 ¾ ounce)
1	**Cup Self-Rising Flour**
1	**Cup Milk**
¾	**Cup Butter**

Spread chopped, cooked chicken in bottom of casserole dish sprayed with cooking spray. Sprinkle chopped boiled eggs over chicken. Mix broth and soup, pour over chicken and eggs. Mix flour, milk and butter until fairly smooth, pour over broth. Bake at 375 degrees for about 45 minutes. If prefer vegetables in chicken pie, can add a vegetable medley of your choice to this before cooking.

Chicken Supreme

6	**Whole Chicken Breast, Deboned, Skinless, Cut In Half**
12	**Slices Bacon**
1	**Small Jar Dried Beef,** *(2 ½ ounce)* **Cut Up Fine**
1	**Can Cream of Mushroom Soup** *(10 ¾ ounce)*
1	**Cup Sour Cream**

Spread cut up dried beef in bottom of a foil lined baking pan. Wrap one slice of bacon around each chicken breast half, place on dried beef. Combine mushroom soup and sour cream, spread over chicken. Cover with foil, cook at 275 degrees for 2 ½ hours. Remove foil, lightly brown. Gravy that is created is great over rice or creamed potatoes. (do not add salt)

Breakfast Burrito

½	**Pound Carroll's Pan Sausage, Browned** (Mild, Medium Or Hot)
5	**Eggs, Beaten Slightly Seasoned with Salt and Pepper to Taste**
2-3	**Cups Cheese, Grated**
4	**Flour Tortillas**

Brown sausage, add eggs, desired seasoning, cook until soft set. Place about ½ cup of Egg and sausage mixture in tortilla, cover with cheese, roll tortilla — ready to eat.

Breakfast Casserole

1	**Pound Carroll's Pan Sausage** **(Mild, Medium, or Hot)**
½	**Pound Bacon, Chopped**
6	**Eggs, Beat Lightly**
8	**Frozen Biscuits, Thawed**
½	**Pound Cheese, Grated**

Brown sausage and bacon, mix with eggs, pour this mixture over biscuits that have been flattened into bottom of a 9 x 13 inch pan coated with cooking spray. Bake at 350 degrees for 35 to 45 minutes, or until brown. Remove from oven, top with grated cheese, let stand 10 minutes. Cut into squares, serve.

Breakfast Casserole II

1	**Pound Carroll's Pan Sausage** (Mild, Medium, or Hot)
6	**Slices Bread**
1	**Cup Sharp Cheese, Grated**
6	**Eggs, Beat Lightly**
2	**Cups Milk**
1	**Teaspoon Dry Mustard**
1	**Teaspoon Salt**
1	**Teaspoon Pepper**

Place bread slices in bottom of well greased 9 X 13 inch pan. Brown the sausage, drain well on paper towels. Spoon browned sausage over bread slices. Sprinkle grated cheese over sausage. Mix eggs, milk, dry mustard, salt and pepper together. Pour this mixture over bread. Cover and refrigerate overnight. Bake at 350 degrees for about 30 minutes. Serve warm.

Breakfast Pizza

½	**Pound Carroll's Pan Sausage, Browned** (Mild, Medium Or Hot)
5	**Eggs, Beaten Slightly**
2-3	**Cups Cheese, Grated**
1	**Package Crescent Dinner Rolls** (8 roll package)

Salt and Pepper to Taste

Spread out crescent rolls in bottom of a greased 9 x 13 inch baking pan. Sprinkle sausage over rolls, pour eggs seasoned with salt and pepper to taste, over browned sausage, cover with grated cheese. Bake at 375 degrees for 11 to 15 minutes, until bottom of rolls are browned and cheese is melted.

Breakfast Pie

½-1 **Pound Carroll's Pan Sausage,
     Browned** (Mild, Medium Or Hot)
8-10 **Eggs, Beaten Slightly**
1-2 **Cups Cheese, Grated**
2   **Frozen Pie Shells,** (unbaked)
Salt and Pepper to Taste

Cook sausage in a medium skillet until browned, drain. Place cooked and drained sausage in bottom of two frozen pie shells, pour eggs that have been beaten lightly and sprinkled with salt and pepper over sausage. Place shredded cheese over eggs, bake in a 350 degree oven until pie crust edges are browned and eggs are set, about 20 minutes.

Marinated Deer Steak

1	**Envelope Dry Onion Mix**
2	**Cup Italian Dressing**
4-8	**Pieces Deer Steak**

Mix onion mix and Italian dressing together. Place deer steak in large baggie, pour marinade mixture over steak. Seal and marinate in refrigerator at least one hour, turning baggie periodically. Grill steak, baste with marinade mixture while grilling.

Fish Taco

4-6 Fish Filets, Grilled Until Done
Monterey Jack Cheese
Lettuce, Shredded
Onions
Soft Flour Tortillas

Crumble grilled fish onto tortilla, top with lettuce, cheese, onions, and mango salsa.

Mango Salsa:
** 2   Jars Sliced Mangos, Drained and**
**   Chopped, Reserve Juice**
** ½   Cup Red Onion, Chopped**
** ½   Cup Yellow Bell Pepper, Chopped**
** ½   Cup Red Bell Pepper, Chopped**
** ½   Cup Celery, Chopped**
Jalapeno Pepper, Seeded and Sliced
Cilantro

FISH TACO (continued)

Stir all salsa ingredients together, add just enough mango juice to moisten. Cover salsa, refrigerate overnight. Serve over fish taco or with crackers.

Special thanks to Rachel Day for sharing this recipe with me on a "Cooking With Hugh" show.

Salmon Patties

1	Can Salmon (15 ounce), Drained, <u>Reserve ¼ Cup Liquid</u>
1	Egg
½	Cup Flour
¼	Teaspoon Black Pepper
1	Teaspoon Baking Powder

Break up drained salmon, remove bones, add egg, mix well. Add flour and black pepper to salmon, stir together. Add baking powder to ¼ cup of reserved salmon liquid (discard extra), stir with fork — should foam and expand to ¾ cup. Add this to salmon mixture. Shape into patties or drop by spoonfuls into hot cooking oil. Cook until golden brown, turn, cook a few minutes more until patties are golden brown on both sides.

Vegetables and Side Dishes

Index

Favorite Recipes:

Title   Page Number

_____

_____

_____

_____

_____

_____

_____

_____

_____

_____

_____

_____

_____

_____

_____

_____

Macaroni and Cheese Surprise

1	**Package Elbow Macaroni** (8 ounce)
1	**Can Cream of Mushroom Soup** (10 ¾ ounce)
¼	**Cup Onion, Finely Chopped**
¼	**Cup Pimientos, Chopped**
¼	**Cup Bell Pepper, Chopped**
1	**Cup Mayonnaise** (Dukes, best for this)
½	**Pound Sharp Cheddar Cheese, Grated**

Cook macaroni according to package directions. Drain. Heat soup, onions, pimientos and bell pepper together, cooking on low heat for 5 to 10 minutes. Add mayonnaise and cheese. Stir cooked macaroni into soup mixture. Pour into a 2 quart baking dish — bake at 350 degrees for about 30 minutes.

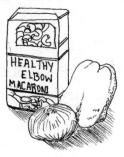

Creamy Brussels Sprouts

4	Cups Brussels Sprouts, Fresh or Frozen
3-4	Cups Chicken Broth
5-6	Slices Bacon
1/4	Cup Onion, Chopped
2	Tablespoons Butter or Olive Oil
1/2	Cup Milk
1/4	Cup Sour Cream
2	Teaspoons All-Purpose Flour
1	Tablespoon Brown Mustard
Salt to Taste	

Cook Brussels sprouts with just enough chicken broth to cover, boil until crisp-tender, about 10 to 12 minutes. Drain. Cook bacon until browned and crisp. Sauté onion in bacon drippings and butter. Combine milk, sour cream, flour, mustard and salt, stir into sautéd onion. Cook and stir until thickened and bubbly. Stir in Brussels sprouts; heat through, serve. Can substitute green beans, just as good.

Baked Beans

1	Can Pork and Beans (20 ounce)
¼	Cup Ketchup
¼	Cup Sugar
2	Tablespoons Mustard
2	Tablespoons Cane Syrup
2	Teaspoons Bacon Drippings
1	Small Onion, Chopped Fine

Salt and Pepper to Taste
Slices of Bacon

Combine all ingredients, except bacon, pour in a greased baking dish. Top with bacon. Bake at 350 degrees for about an hour until bacon is cooked and browned, serve.

Parmesan Tomatoes

6   **Roma Tomatoes**
1   **Cup Italian Dressing**
2   **Tablespoons Worcestershire Sauce**
½   **Cup Parmesan Cheese**
Salt to Taste

Cut Roma tomatoes in half, arrange, cut side up, in a greased baking dish. Sprinkle tomatoes with salt to taste. Mix Italian dressing and Worcestershire sauce together, pour over tomatoes. Cover tomatoes with parmesan cheese. Bake at 375 degrees for about 15 minutes, or until tomatoes are tender. Great served as a side dish with grilled steak.

Tomatoes And Okra

4	**Tomatoes, Peeled and Cut Into Chunks**
1	**Cup Okra, Cut Into ½ inch Slices**
½	**Cup Onion, Chopped**
3	**Tablespoons Butter or Bacon Drippings**
1	**Teaspoon Salt**
½	**Teaspoon Pepper**

Sauté okra and onion in butter over low heat. Add tomatoes, salt and pepper. Cook until all vegetables are tender, stirring occasionally. Great served over rice.

Fried Okra

1   Pound Okra
2   Cups Self-Rising Flour
1½ Cups Buttermilk
Vegetable Oil
Salt to Taste

Wash okra, drain well, remove stem end and tips. Cut okra into ½ inch slices. Pour buttermilk over okra, coating okra well. Wait 10 or 15 minutes, then dredge okra in flour. Fry okra in 375 degree oil until browned. Drain on paper towel, salt and pepper to taste.

Broccoli Casserole

1	**Package Frozen Chopped Broccoli** *(16 ounce)*
1	**Can Cream of Mushroom Soup** *(10 ¾ ounce)*
1	**Cup Sharp Cheese, Grated**
¾	**Cup Mayonnaise**
¼	**Cup Onion, Chopped**
1	**Egg**

Cracker Crumbs

2	**Tablespoons Butter**

Cook broccoli about 5 minutes in microwave, stirring after 2 minutes. Drain, add all remaining ingredients, except cracker crumbs and butter, mix well. Pour in a greased baking dish, sprinkle cracker crumbs on top of broccoli mixture, dot with butter. Bake at 350 degrees for 30 minutes.

Easy Broccoli Casserole

2	**Cups Long-Grain Rice**
	(Cooked according to package directions)
16	**Ounce Package Chopped Broccoli**
	(Cooked according to package directions)
2	**Cans Cream of Mushroom Soup**
	(10 ¾ ounce)
1	**Pound Velveeta Cheese, Cubed**
1	**Cup Cracker Crumbs**
2	**Tablespoons Butter, Melted**

Mix cooked rice, cooked broccoli, soup and cubed Velveeta together. Pour into a greased shallow baking dish. Combine cracker crumbs and melted butter then sprinkle over casserole. Bake at 350 degrees for 30 minutes until cheese is melted, casserole is bubbly and top is slightly browned.

Butter Beans

1-2 **Cups Frozen Butterbeans**
(Speckled, Green, Dark, Etc.)
3 ½ **Cups Water**
Ham Hocks (or seasoning of your choice)
1 **Teaspoon Sugar**
Salt and Pepper to Taste

Bring water to a boil, add ham hocks or season-ing of your choice and frozen butterbeans.

Bring back to a boil, add sugar, salt and pepper. Reduce heat, cover and simmer for about 30 minutes or until beans are desired doneness.

Candied Yams

6   Large Sweet Potatoes
2   Cups Sugar
1   Cup Butter
2   Tablespoons Vanilla Flavoring

Wash and peel sweet potatoes, cut into 1 inch inch slices, place in a greased baking dish, top with sugar, butter and flavoring. Bake uncovered at 350 degrees for about one hour.

Sweet Potato Soufflé

3   Cups Sweet Potatoes, Cooked and
       Mashed
1   Cup Sugar
½   Cup Butter
1   Teaspoon Vanilla
½   Teaspoon Salt
2   Eggs
Milk (optional)

Whip sweet potatoes until fluffy. Add all other in-gredients. May need to add some milk, if too thick. Pour into a greased baking dish, add nut topping.

Topping:
1   Cup Pecans, Chopped
1   Cup Brown Sugar
⅓   Cup Flour
⅓   Cup Margarine

Mix all ingredients, sprinkle on top of sweet po-tato mixture. Bake at 325 degrees for 30 to 45 minutes until topping is browned and potatoes are set.

Baked Cream Potatoes

8-10 Potatoes
8 Ounce Cream Cheese
1 Cup Sour Cream
½ Cup Butter
1 Teaspoon Salt
Cheddar Cheese, Grated

Cook potatoes until tender, mash. Add butter, cream cheese, sour cream and salt, beat together. Pour in a greased 9 x 13 inch baking dish, sprinkle with grated cheese. Bake at 350 degrees for 30 to 45 minutes.

Cheesy Potatoes

4	Medium Potatoes, Peeled, Sliced and Cooked
1	Cup Milk
1/4	Cup Butter
2	Tablespoons Flour
1 1/2	Cup Cheddar Cheese, Grated

Combine milk, butter, and flour. Cook over medium heat until mixture begins to thicken, stirring often, forming a white sauce. Add salt and pepper. Place sliced and cooked potatoes in a greased casserole dish, pour white sauce over potatoes, bake uncovered in 350 degree oven for 20 to 25 minutes. Take from oven, cover potatoes with grated cheese, place back in oven for 5 to 10 minutes.

Potato Salad

6	Medium Potatoes
3	Eggs, Hard Boiled, Chopped
½	Cup Mayonnaise
¼	Cup Pickle Relish, Sweet or Dill
¼	Cup Onion, Chopped
1	Tablespoon Yellow Mustard

Salt and Pepper to Taste

Peel potatoes, cut into 1-inch cubes. Cover potatoes with water in a large saucepan, bring to a boil. Cook potatoes until tender (cracks when fork inserted). Drain. Add eggs, mayonnaise, relish, onion, mustard, salt and pepper to potatoes. Mix gently. Great served warm or cold.

Roasted Red Potatoes

10-12 New Red Potatoes, Cut in Half
1   Clove Garlic, Minced
¼   Cup Olive Oil
¼   Cup Butter, Melted
1   Teaspoon Onion Salt
½   Teaspoon Dill Weed
½   Teaspoon Paprika
¼   Teaspoon Black Pepper

Mix all ingredients above, making sure that potatoes are coated well. Bake on foil lined baking sheet at 350 degrees for 25 to 30 minutes, or until potatoes are done.

Twice Baked Potatoes

4	**Large Baking Potatoes, Baked**
¼	**Cup Butter**
¼	**Cup Sour Cream**
3-4	**Tablespoons Milk**
½	**Cup Cheddar Cheese, Grated**

Bacon Bits, Optional
Salt and Pepper to Taste

Cut baked potatoes in half, lengthwise. Scoop potato out, leaving skin, mix potato with sour cream, butter, and milk. Mix well, mashing potato with a fork. Salt and pepper to taste. Spoon potato mixture back into potato skins, place on foil lined baking sheet, top potatoes with grated cheese, bake at 350 degrees for 10 to 15 minutes until potatoes thoroughly heated and cheese melts. Garnish with bacon bits. Can substitute ranch dressing for sour cream and milk.

Hash Brown Potato Casserole

32	**Ounce Package Hash Brown Potatoes** (semi-thawed)
2	**Cups Cheese, Grated**
2	**Cups Sour Cream**
1/2	**Cup Onion, Chopped**
1/2	**Cup Butter, Melted**
1	**Teaspoon Salt**
1/2	**Teaspoon Black Pepper**
1	**Can Cream of Mushroom Soup** (10 3/4 ounce)

Mix all ingredients together. Bake at 350 degrees for about one hour. Can top with cracker crumbs or crushed corn flakes before cooking, if desired.

Hopping John

2 **Cups Fresh Black Eye Peas,
Cooked and Drained [or 2 (10 ounce)
Packages Frozen]**
½ **Cup White Rice, Uncooked**
4 **Strips Bacon, Chopped**
¼ **Cup Onions, Chopped**
2 **Cups Water**
Salt and Black Pepper to Taste

Cook bacon and onions over medium heat until bacon is crisp and onion is clear. Add peas and rice, then water. Cover and simmer over low heat about 20 minutes, or until rice is done. Salt and pepper to taste.

Fried Black Eye Peas Patties

1   Cup Self-Rising Flour
1   Cup Black Eye Peas, Cooked and
        Drained
½   Cup Milk
1   Teaspoon Salt
½   Teaspoon Black Pepper
1   Egg

Combine all ingredients, stir together until thick, but able to spoon out (may need to add more milk or water until right consistency). Drop by spoonfuls into hot grease, fry 2 to 3 minutes on each side until golden brown. Can add crumbled bacon or chopped peppers or onions for added flavor.

Thanks Lynn Brady for this recipe.

Green Beans

1½ Pounds Fresh or Frozen Italian Cut Green Beans
¼ Cup Butter
1 Tablespoon Olive Oil
½ Teaspoon Garlic Salt
½ Teaspoon Celery Salt

Melt butter in preheated pan, add olive oil, salts, stir. Add green beans that have been washed, stir to coat with butter and oil mixture, cover and simmer 10 to 15 minutes until desired tenderness. Beans should contain enough water, so should not need to add more.

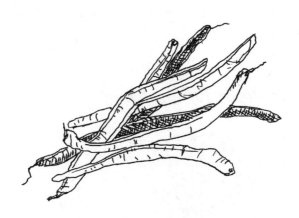

Cooking With Hugh

Green Bean Casserole

Green Beans *(20 - 28 ounce)*
1   **Can Cream of Mushroom Soup**
      (10 ¾ ounce)
¾   **Cup Milk**
1   **Can French-Fried Onion Rings**
      (2.8 ounce)
Pepper to Taste

Combine drained green beans with soup, milk and pepper, add half of the onion rings. Pour into a greased glass baking dish. Bake at 350 degrees for 30 minutes, until heated through and bubbly, top with remaining onion rings, cook additional 5 minutes. A great old favorite.

Green Beans, Southern Style

2   **Strip Bacon, Cut Up**
2   **Tablespoons Onion, Chopped**
1   **Tablespoon Flour**
1   **Quart Canned Green Beans, Drained** (reserve liquid)
Salt and Pepper to Taste

Lightly fry bacon, add onion, sauté together until bacon is crisp. Blend in flour, salt and pepper. Drain half of the liquid from beans into bacon drippings. Stir well. Add beans and heat thoroughly. Serve

Onion Rings

2-3 Large Onions
½   Cup Corn Starch
½   Cup Flour
1   Teaspoon Baking Powder
½   Cup Water
1   Egg
Salt and Pepper to Taste

Preheat oil to 375 degrees, slice onions into ½ to ¾ inch slices. Separate rings. Mix dry ingredients together in medium-sized mixing bowl. Add water and egg, mixing well. Dip sliced rings into batter and drop into hot grease. Fry for 3 to 4 minutes on each side until golden brown. Drain on paper towels and sprinkle with salt.

Grilled Vegetables

1	Medium Baking Potato, Cut Into Wedges
1	Green Bell Pepper, Cut in Half, Seeds Removed
1	Red Bell Pepper, Cut in Half, Seeds Removed
2	Yellow Squash, Sliced About ½ inch Thick
2	Roma Tomatoes, Cut in Half
½	Cup Italian Dressing
1	Teaspoon Coarse Ground Black Pepper
½	Teaspoon Garlic Powder
½	Teaspoon Celery Salt
½	Teaspoon Salt

Mix Italian dressing, garlic powder, salts, and pepper together until blended. Pour over vegetables in a large plastic bag, making sure all are coated. Refrigerate about 10 to 15 minutes. Grill vegetables on cooking spray coated rack, with lid closed, over medium to medium-high heat,

---

basting with dressing mixture. Potato wedges should be grilled about 20 to 25 minutes, or until tender, squash should be grilled about 3 to 4 minutes on each side, or until tender. Tomatoes and peppers should be grilled, 3 to 5 minutes or until skin begins to split.

Grilled Corn

4   **Medium Ears of Corn, Shucked with Silks Removed**

½   **Cup Butter, Melted**

½   **Teaspoon Coarse Ground Black Pepper**

¼-½ **Teaspoon Celery Salt**

¼-½ **Teaspoon Salt**

Grill shucked corn on cooking spray coated rack, with lid closed, over medium to medium-high heat, turning corn as needed. Cook 10 to 15 minutes until corn is brown speckled and done to taste. Mix celery salt, pepper and salt together in melted butter until blended. Pour over cooked corn — serve.

Pineapple Casserole

2	**Cans Pineapple Tidbits** (20 ounce), **Drained, Reserve Juice**
¾	**Cup Sugar**
6	**Tablespoons Flour**
½	**Cup Butter, Melted**
2	**Cups Sharp Cheese, Grated** **Cracker Crumbs**

Mix sugar, flour and six tablespoons of pineapple juice together. Add pineapple, butter and cheese, mix well. Pour into a glass baking dish sprayed with cooking spray, top with cracker crumbs, bake at 325 degrees for about 30 to 45 minutes.

Pineapple Marshmallow Casserole

1	**Can Pineapple Tidbits** (20 ounce), **Drained, Reserve Juice**
8	**Ounces Cream Cheese, Cubed**
1	**Cup Miniature Marshmallows**
½	**Cup Sugar**
2	**Tablespoons Flour**
1	**Egg**
½	**Cup Sharp Cheese, Grated**

Mix sugar, flour, egg and pineapple juice. Cook in a double boiler or in the microwave, stirring often, until thickened. Cool slightly. Place pineapple tidbits, topped with cubed cream cheese and marshmallows, in a greased 8 x 8 inch baking dish. Pour pineapple juice mixture over pineapple, cream cheese, and marshmallows. Sprinkle with grated cheese. Bake at 450 degrees for about 10 minutes, until cheese has melted and mixture is bubbly.

Rutabagas

3   **Small Rutabagas**
3   **Cups Water**
¼   **Cup Butter**
Salt and Pepper to Taste

Peel rutabagas and cut into bite size pieces. Place in just enough water to cover, add butter, salt and pepper. Bring water to a boil, reduce heat, cover and simmer for 1 to 1 ½ hours, or until rutabagas are tender. Can season with bacon drippings if desired.

Summer Squash – Fried

**1   Pound Yellow Squash, Cut into
      ¼ inch slices**
½-1 Cup Corn Meal Mix
Vegetable Oil
Salt and Pepper to Taste

Dredge sliced squash in corn meal mix. Cook slices in 375 degree oil, turning to brown both sides. Drain on paper towels, salt and pepper to desired taste.

Squash Casserole

3-4	Cups Squash, Sliced, Cooked and Drained
1	Cup Cheese, Grated
1	Cup Sour Cream
2	Tablespoons Onion, Grated
2	Carrots, Grated
1	Can Cream of Chicken Soup (10 ¾ ounce)
1	Package Stuffing Mix (8 ounce)
½	Cup Butter, Melted
1	Jar Pimiento (2 ounce), Optional

Mix stuffing mix and butter, set aside. Add all remaining ingredients to drained cooked squash. Place half of stuffing/ butter mixture in bottom of a glass dish sprayed with cooking spray. Pour squash mixture next, top with remaining stuffing/butter mixture. Bake in 375 degree oven for about 30 minutes. Can add drained chopped pimiento to squash mixture before cooking for added color.

Squash Casserole II

2	Pounds Yellow Squash, Sliced, Cooked and Drained
1	Cup Onion, Chopped
3	Eggs
½	Cup Ritz Crackers, Crumbled
½	Cup Sour Cream
½	Cup Mayonnaise
¾	Cup Milk
1	Envelope Hidden Valley Original Buttermilk Dressing Mix (.4 ounces)
1	Cup Cheese, Grated
2	Cups Ritz Crackers, Crumbled
2	Tablespoons Butter, Melted

Cook squash and onion in salted water until tender. Drain. Mix eggs, ½ cup cracker crumbs, mayonnaise, sour cream, milk, Buttermilk Dressing Mix and cheese together, fold into squash and onion mixture. Pour into a two quart baking dish. Top with 2 cups cracker crumbs mixed with melted butter. Bake at 375 degrees for 30 to 40 minutes, until set and lightly browned.

Eggplant Casserole

2	Medium Eggplants, Peeled and Cubed
1	Cup Onion, Chopped
½	Cup Celery, Chopped
½	Stick Butter
¼	Cup Flour
1	Cup Milk
1	Egg, Beaten
2	Tablespoons Parmesan Cheese

Boil eggplant in salted water just until tender. Drain and place in a shallow baking dish. Sauté onion and celery in ½ stick butter. Add flour and milk to onion/celery mixture, blending well. Cook until thickened. Remove from heat, stir in egg. Pour over eggplant. Combine cracker crumbs, Parmesan cheese and the 2 tablespoons melted butter. Sprinkle over casserole. Bake at 375 degrees for 25 minutes or until bubbly and browned.

Turnip Greens

1	**Bunch Fresh Turnip Greens** *(with or without roots)*
2-3	**Cups Water**
2	**Tablespoons Salt**
1	**Tablespoons Sugar**
¼	**Pound Salt Pork**

Make sure that greens have been washed thoroughly and are free from grit. Boil salt pork, sugar, and salt in water for about 30 minutes. Add greens to boiling water, cover and simmer an additional 2 hours. Serve with cornbread.

Vegetables – Southern Style

2   Cups Shelled Peas or Butterbeans
1   Piece Pork Seasoning Meat
1   Teaspoon Sugar
Water
Salt to Taste

Use as little water as possible, need to just cover vegetable — bring water to a boil, add salt, sugar and seasoning meat (can substitute one tablespoon of bacon drippings for meat). Add vegetables, return to a boil. Reduce heat, cover and simmer 30 to 45 minutes, cook only until vegetables are tender.

If cutting back on calories and fat, you can substitute two chicken bouillon cubes for pork meat, not quite as good, but very tasty.

Brown Rice

½	Cup Butter
1	Small Onion, Diced
1	Cup Raw Rice
1	Can Beef Consommé (10 ¾ ounce)
1	Soup Can Water
1	Can Sliced Mushrooms (6.5 ounce)

Melt butter, add diced onion. Mix rice, beef consommé, water and mushrooms with butter and onion. Pour into cooking spray coated baking dish. Bake uncovered at 350 degrees for about one hour or until liquid is absorbed.

Bacon-Wrapped Asparagus

1   **Pound Asparagus, Washed**
1   **Pound Bacon**
½   **Stick Butter, Melted**
1   **Tablespoons Lemon Juice**
Salt and Pepper

Trim asparagus by snapping off woody ends. Create bundles of 3 stalks of asparagus each. Wrap each bundle with 1 slice bacon, starting at non-flowered end (flower should be exposed at other end). Place in oven-safe dish. Combine melted butter and lemon juice and drizzle over asparagus. Sprinkle with salt and black pepper to taste. Bake at 350 degrees for 15 to 20 minutes, or until bacon is done.

Pasta Vegetable Medley

1	Package Pasta, Cooked and Drained
2	Cups Diced, Smoked Ham
1	Medium Tomato, Diced
1/2	Medium Onion, Diced
1	Cup Diced Bell Pepper (any color)
1	Small Zucchini, Washed and Diced
1	Cup Sliced, Fresh Mushrooms
1/2	Cup Sliced Black Olives
1/4	Cup Capers
3/4	Cup Parmesan Cheese
1	Stick Butter
2	Tablespoons Olive Oil

Salt and Pepper

In a large skillet, sautee ham and next seven ingredients in butter and olive oil over medium heat until tender. Remove from heat. Combine pasta, vegetables, and parmesan cheese in a large bowl. Salt and pepper to taste. Serve warm.

Makes a really pretty dish served in a large glass bowl. Serves 10 to 12.

Breads, Biscuits and Muffins

Index

Favorite Recipes:

Title   Page Number

_____

_____

_____

_____

_____

_____

_____

_____

_____

_____

_____

_____

_____

_____

_____

Done and Buttered Biscuits

2	Cups Bisquick
1	Cup Sour Cream
½	Cup Butter, Melted

Mix Bisquick and sour cream. Add melted butter, mix well. Fill greased muffin tins about three-fourths full, bake in a 425 degree oven for 10 minutes.

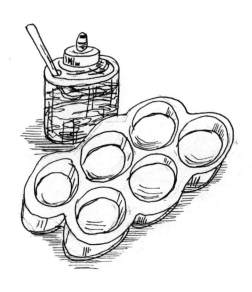

Pancakes

2	Cups Bisquick
1	Cup Milk
2	Eggs
2	Tablespoons Lemon Juice
1	Tablespoon Sugar
2	Teaspoons Baking Powder

Mix all ingredients, batter should be slightly lumpy. For 3 inch diameter pancakes, pour approximately ¼ cup batter on a heated buttered griddle. When you can see bubbles on top side of pancake, time to turn.

French Toast For 2

4   **Slices Bread**
2   **Tablespoons Butter**
2   **Eggs**
2   **Tablespoons Milk**
Dash of Salt

Melt butter in frying pan over medium-high heat. Beat together eggs, milk and salt. Dip bread slices into egg mixture, place in skillet and brown each side. Serve with powdered sugar or syrup.

Onion and Sour Cream Cornbread

1	Cup Onion, Chopped
2	Tablespoons Brown Sugar
3	Tablespoons Oil (divided)
1	Cup Sour Cream
2/3	Cup Milk
1	Egg, Beaten
2	Tablespoons Butter, Melted
2	Cups Self-Rising Corn Meal Mix

In a large skillet, cook and stir onion and sugar in 2 tablespoons of oil over medium heat until onions are tender and lightly browned. Set aside to cool. Place 1 tablespoon oil in an iron skillet, heat skillet in a preheated 375 degree oven for 10 minutes. In a large bowl, combine sour cream, milk, egg and butter, add onions. Stir in cornmeal mix, until moistened. Pour batter into hot skillet and bake for 20 to 25 minutes.

Fried Lace Bread

½   **Cup Self-Rising Corn Meal Mix**
½   **Cup Water**

Mix water with corn meal mix. Let stand for 2 to 3 minutes to slightly thicken. Pour small amount of corn meal mixture into heavy skillet with ¼ to ½ inch hot grease. Cook about 2 minutes on each side until golden brown, turning once. May need to add more water or more corn meal mix — the thinner the mixture, the lacier the bread, but grease will also pop more, use caution.

Grilled Garlic Bread

1	**Loaf French Bread, Split Horizontally**
¼-½	**Cup Butter, Melted**
½-¾	**Cup Parmesan Cheese**
½	**Teaspoon Garlic Salt**

Toast bread on grill, cut side down, until golden brown. Brush toasted bread with melted butter, sprinkle with garlic salt and parmesan cheese. Place cut sides together. Wrap loaf in aluminum foil, place back on grill for 15 minutes or until bread is completely warmed.

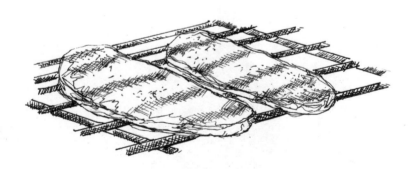

Grilled Tomato Cheese Bread

1   **Loaf French Bread, Split Horizontally Butter, Melted**
1   **Glove Garlic, Minced**
Sliced Mozzarella Cheese
Tomatoes, Sliced Very Thin
Garlic Salt

Toast bread on grill, cut side down, until golden brown, meanwhile melt butter, add garlic to butter. Spread garlic butter on cut side of toasted bread. Layer mozzarella cheese on bread, top with thinly cut tomatoes. Place bread on pan in a preheated 350 degree oven for about 10 to 15 minutes until bread is completely warmed, cheese is melted and tomatoes are cooked.

Sweet Potato Biscuits

2   **Cups Self-Rising Flour**
2   **Tablespoons Sugar**
⅓   **Cup Butter**
1   **Cup Sweet Potatoes, Cooked and Mashed**
¾-1   **Cup Buttermilk**

Mix flour and sugar together. Cut in butter and add sweet potatoes. Stir in milk to make a stiff dough. Kneed dough a few times on flour covered cloth. Pinch a small amount off and roll between palms to form a ball, then flatten onto a greased cookie sheet or can roll the dough out to about ½ inch thick and cut with a biscuit cutter. Bake in a 450 degree oven about 10 to 15 minutes or until golden brown.

Blueberry Muffins

½	**Cup Butter, Melted**
1	**Egg**
½	**Cup Milk**
1¾	**Cups Plain Flour**
¾	**Cup Sugar**
2½	**Teaspoons Baking Powder**
¼	**Teaspoon Salt**
1	**Cup Blueberries**

Melt butter in measuring cup, add egg and milk. Sift dry ingredients together. Add butter mixture to dry ingredients. Mix well. Add blueberries. Pour into greased muffin tin. Bake at 400 degrees for 20 to 25 minutes.

Mayonnaise Muffins

2	**Cups Self-Rising Flour**
1	**Cup Milk**
¼	**Cup Mayonnaise**
2	**Teaspoons Sugar**

Combine all ingredients, mix well. Spoon into greased muffin tins. Bake in 400 degree oven for 10 to 20 minutes or until brown.

Sausage Muffins

½   **Pound Carroll's Pan Sausage**
      (Mild, Medium or Hot), Browned

1   **Cup Self-Rising Flour**

1   **Cup Sour Cream**

½   **Cup Butter, Softened**

½   **Cup Sharp Cheese, Grated**

Mix flour, sour cream and butter. Add grated cheese. Add cooked and drained sausage. Pour into greased muffin tins, bake at 350 degrees for 15 to 20 minutes.

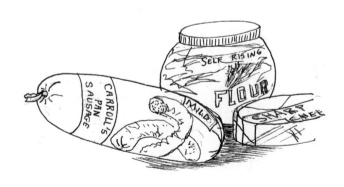

Sour Cream Muffins

1   **Cup Self-Rising Flour**
½   **Cup Sour Cream**
½   **Cup Butter, Melted**

Mix flour and sour cream into melted butter. Spoon into greased muffin tins. Bake at 400 degrees for about 10 to 15 minutes or until brown.

Easy Dinner Muffins

1	**Cup Self-Rising Flour**
¾	**Cups Buttermilk**
2	**Tablespoons Oil**
¼	**Cup Melted Butter**

Preheat oven to 425 degrees. Mix together flour, buttermilk, and oil and spoon into ungreased muffin tins. Bake 15 minutes. Brush tops of muffins with melted butter.

Try serving with Sweet Garlic Butter Sauce (page 60).

Fried Cheese Biscuits

6   Frozen Southern-Style Biscuits,
        Thawed Or 1 Can Southern Style
        Biscuits
Sharp Cheddar Cheese, Cut Into
        12 1Inch Cubes
Oil

Cut biscuits in half. On a floured surface, roll biscuit halves out to $\frac{1}{3}$ inch thickness. Place one cube cheese in center of biscuit half. Wrap biscuit around cheese sealing edges. Drop into hot grease and fry 4 to 5 minutes or until biscuits are golden brown.

Try adding a small piece of fried bacon to cheese. Like a bite-size bacon and cheese biscuit. Really good for breakfast.

Cakes, Candies, Cookies and Desserts

Index

Favorite Recipes:

Title   Page Number

_____

_____

_____

_____

_____

_____

_____

_____

_____

_____

_____

_____

_____

_____

_____

_____

Dump Cake

2	**Large Cans Crushed Pineapple** (20 ounce)
1	**Box White Cake Mix** (18¼ ounce)
½	**Cup Butter**
2	**Cups Toasted Pecans**

Preheat oven to 350 degrees. Grease bottom of 9 x 13 inch baking dish. Drain 1 can pineapple and discard juice. Dump both cans (drained and undrained) in bottom of pan. Dump dry cake mix in pan over pineapple. Drop butter by ½ teaspoons over top of cake mix. Sprinkle with pecans and bake for 45 to 50 minutes.

This is very quick and easy to make. Serve with ice cream as a topping while cake is still warm, delicious.

Hawaiian Dump Cake

1	**Can Coconut** (3 ½ ounce)
1	**Can Crushed Pineapple** (20 ounce)
1	**Box Yellow Cake Mix** (18 ¼ ounce)
1	**Cup Butter**
½	**Cup Pecans**

Preheat oven to 350 degrees. Grease bottom of 9 x 13 inch baking dish. Layer the coconut, then the undrained pineapple. Sprinkle the dry cake mix over the pineapple. Dot with butter slices and sprinkle with nuts.

Bake for 30 to 35 minutes until golden brown. Cut in squares, serve coconut side up. Great topped with ice cream.

Earthquake Cake

1	**Cup Pecans**
1	**Can Coconut** (3 ½ ounce)
1	**Box German Chocolate Cake Mix** (18 ¼ ounce)

Grease bottom of a 9 X 13 inch baking dish. Sprinkle pecans and coconut in bottom of dish.
Mix the German Chocolate Cake Mix according to directions on box. Pour over pecans and coconut.

8	**Ounces Cream Cheese, Softened**
½	**Cup Butter**
1	**Box Powdered Sugar, Sifted**
1	**Teaspoon Vanilla**

Beat cream cheese and butter together, with electric mixer, gradually add sugar and vanilla, continuing to beat. Drop spoonfuls of cream cheese/butter mixture on top of cake batter. Bake at 350 degrees for about 45 minutes. Let set for 30 minutes before cutting into squares.

30 Minute Fudge Cake

2   **Cups Sugar**
1 ½   **Cups Self-Rising Flour, Sifted**
1   **Cup Butter**
½   **Cup Cocoa**
1   **Teaspoon Vanilla Flavoring**
4   **Eggs**
Miniature Marshmallows

Combine all ingredients, except marshmallows. Beat well, pour into a greased 9 x 13 inch baking dish. Bake at 350 degrees for 25 minutes. Remove from oven and cover top with marshmallows while cake is still hot. Cover marshmallows with frosting.

Frosting

½	**Cup Butter**
1/3	**Cup Milk**
½	**Cup Cocoa**
1	**Pound Box Powdered Sugar**
1	**Teaspoon Vanilla Flavoring**
Chopped Nuts	

Heat milk and butter in microwave until butter has melted. Add sugar, cocoa and vanilla, beat well. Spread over marshmallows. Garnish with chopped nuts.

This is an old favorite and is very similar to Mississippi Mud. If you love chocolate and have a sweet tooth, this is the cake for you. This recipe calls for ½ cup cocoa in frosting, but I usually cut that back a little, maybe between 1/3 and ½ cup, not quite so chocolaty.

Easy Banana Nut Cake

1	**Package Yellow Cake Mix** *(18 ¼ ounce)*
1	**Package Butter Pecan Instant Pudding** *(3 ounce)*
4	**Eggs**
1	**Cup Water**
½	**Cup Bananas, Mashed**
¼	**Cup Vegetable Oil**
½	**Cup Chopped Nuts, Pecans or Walnuts**

Blend all ingredients together, except nuts, beat 3 or 4 minutes, until smooth. Add nuts, stir, pour into tube pan. Bake at 350 degrees for about 45 to 50 minutes.

No Bake Fruit Cake

4	**Cups Pecans, Chopped**
1	**Box Vanilla Wafers** (12 ounce), **Crushed**
1	**Small Box Raisins** (15 ounce)
1	**Can Sweetened Condensed Milk** (14 ounce)
½	**Cup Candied Cherries, Chopped**

Combine all ingredients, place in spring-form pan. Refrigerate. (Best if entire box of wafers is not added, you do not want cake to be too dry.)

Peach Pound Cake

1 ½	Cups Vegetable Oil
2	Cups Sugar
3	Eggs
2	Teaspoons Vanilla Flavoring
3	Cups Self-Rising Flour
3	Cups Ripe Peaches, Peeled and Chopped
1	Cup Nuts, Chopped
½	Cup Coconut

Mix oil, sugar, eggs and flavoring. Add flour, mix well. Fold in peaches, nuts and coconut. Pour into a greased tube pan and bake one hour at 350 degrees.

Can substitute apples or pears for peaches. Very good served warm topped with ice cream.

Best-Ever Pound Cake

1	**Pound Butter**
3	**Cups Sugar**
8	**Eggs**
3	**Cups All-Purpose** (Plain) **Flour**
½	**Cup Whole Milk**
1	**Teaspoon Vanilla Flavoring**
1	**Teaspoon Lemon Flavoring**

Cream butter and sugar until fluffy. Add eggs, one at a time, beating well after each egg is added. Add flour and milk alternately, beginning and ending with flour. Add flavorings. Pour into greased and floured tube pan and bake in a pre-heated 325 degree oven for about 90 minutes, or until knife inserted in center comes out clean.

Cream Cheese Pound Cake

3 **Sticks Butter** (1 ½ Cups)
3 **Cups Sugar**
3 **Cups Plain Flour**
6 **Eggs**
8 **Ounce Package Cream Cheese**
½ **Teaspoon Salt**
1 **Tablespoon Vanilla Flavoring**

Cream butter and sugar together. Add eggs to butter mixture, one at a time, continuing to beat well after each egg is added. Add flour, salt and vanilla flavoring, beating at low speed. Pour into greased and floured tube pan and bake in a pre-heated 300 degree oven for about 1 ½ hours, or until knife inserted in center comes out clean.

Perfect Pound Cake

1	**Cup Butter**
½	**Cup Shortening**
5	**Eggs**
3	**Cups Sugar**
3	**Cups Plain Flour**
½	**Teaspoon Baking Powder**
½	**Teaspoon Salt**
1	**Cup Milk**
1	**Tablespoon Vanilla Flavoring**

Cream butter and shortening together. Add sugar and eggs to butter mixture, continuing to beat. Sift dry ingredients together, add alternately with milk to creamed mixture. Add vanilla flavoring. Pour into greased and floured tube pan and bake in a preheated 325 degree oven for about 1 ½ hours, or until knife inserted in center comes out clean.

Sour Cream Pound Cake

2	**Sticks Butter**
3	**Cups Sugar**
3	**Cups Cake Flour, Sifted**
6	**Eggs**
8	**Ounces Sour Cream**
¼	**Teaspoon Baking Soda**
I	**Teaspoon Vanilla Flavoring**

Cream butter and sugar together. Add eggs to butter mixture, one at a time, beating well after each egg is added (about one minute, should be light and fluffy). Sift flour and soda together, add to butter/egg mixture, continuing to beat at low speed. Add sour cream and vanilla. Pour into greased and floured tube pan and bake in a pre-heated 300 degree oven for about I ½ hours, or until knife inserted in center comes out clean.

Pineapple Cake

1	**Box Yellow Cake Mix** *(18¼ ounce)*
1	**Small Can Crushed Pineapple** *(6 ½ ounce)*
4	**Eggs**
1	**Cup Vegetable Oil**

Combine all ingredients, including pineapple juice, mix well. Pour into three 8 inch greased and floured round cake pans. Bake in a 350 degree oven about 20 to 25 minutes or until browned and knife inserted in center comes out clean. Cool completely before frosting.

Frosting

1	**Large Can Crushed Pineapple** *(20 ounce)*
1	**Container Whipped Topping** *(16 ounce)*
1	**Box Vanilla Instant Pudding** *(3 ounce)*

Mix all ingredients together, including pineapple juice, mix well. Frost cake, keep refrigerated.

Tropical Island Cake

Filling:

8	**Ounces Coconut**
1	**Cup Sour Cream**
2	**Cups Sugar**
1	**Can Crushed Pineapple** (20 ounce), **Drained**

Mix all ingredients together, refrigerate until cake has baked and has cooled.

Cake Batter:

1	**Box Butter Cake Mix** (18¼ ounce)
4	**Eggs**
1	**Cup Sour Cream**
½	**Cup Crisco Oil**
¼	**Cup Water**
¼	**Cup Sugar**

Combine cake mix, eggs, sour cream, oil, water and sugar, mixing well. Pour batter into 3 cake pans, bake in a preheated 350 degree oven for about 20 minutes or until layers are golden brown. Cool.

Frosting

1	**Large Can Crushed Pineapple** (20 ounce)
1	**Container Whipped Topping** (16 ounce)
1	**Box Vanilla Instant Pudding** (3 ounce)

Mix all ingredients together, including pineapple juice, mix well.

When cake layers have cooled, spoon filling between layers and cover with frosting. Keep refrigerated.

Caramel Cake

2	Cups Sugar
1	Cup Butter
4	Eggs
1	Cup Milk
3	Cups All-Purpose (Plain) Flour
2	Teaspoons Baking Powder
1	Teaspoon Vanilla Flavoring
1	Teaspoon Lemon Flavoring

Beat sugar and butter until light and fluffy, add eggs, beating well. Add milk and dry ingredients, then flavorings. Pour batter into 4 round cake pans coated with cooking spray and bake in a preheated 350 degree oven for about 20 minutes or until layers are golden brown. Let layers cool, then cover with icing.

CARAMEL CAKE (continued)

Caramel Icing
   3 ½ Cups Sugar
   1   Cup Evaporated Milk
   ½   Cup Butter

Brown ½ cup of sugar in a heavy saucepan. Remove pan from heat and add remaining 3 cups of sugar, milk and butter. Mix well, but try to avoid splattering sugar on sides of pan. Return to heat, bring to a boil, then continue boiling on medium heat for additional 12 minutes. Remove from heat and let cool down slightly before icing cake.

Sour Cream Coffee Cake

½	**Cup Pecans, Chopped**
¼	**Cup Brown Sugar**
2	**Teaspoons Cinnamon**

Combine ingredients above; set aside.

1	**Box Yellow Cake Mix** (18¼ ounce)
1	**Cup Sour Cream**
⅔	**Cup Vegetable Oil**
½	**Cup Sugar**
4	**Eggs**
1	**Teaspoon Vanilla Flavoring**
½	**Cup Pecans, Chopped**

Combine cake mix, sour cream, oil, sugar, eggs and vanilla. Beat 2 minutes, stir in pecans. Pour half the batter into a lightly greased and floured tube pan. Sprinkle brown sugar mixture over batter, pour remaining batter into pan over brown sugar mixture. Bake in 325 degree oven for 1 hour.

Chocolate Covered Marshmallows

1   **Cup Chocolate Chips**
¼   **Cup Shortening** (not margarine)
Large Marshmallows
Wooden Candy Sticks
Optional:
Toasted Coconut
Candy Sprinkles
Chopped Nuts

Heat chocolate chips and shortening at medium heat in microwave for 1 to 4 minutes (stirring often), until chips and shortening has melted. Stir until smooth. Insert candy sticks into marshmallows, dip marshmallows in chocolate. Then roll in nuts, coconut or sprinkles if desired. Cool on waxed paper.

Easy Christmas Candy

24 Ounce Vanilla-Flavored Candy Bark

8-10 Peppermint Candy Canes, Crushed

Heat vanilla candy bark at medium heat in microwave for 1 to 4 minutes, stirring every 30 seconds, until candy has melted. Stir until smooth then stir in crushed peppermint. Pour onto waxed paper, spread thinly. After cooled, break into pieces.

Martha Washington Candy

2	**Pounds Confectioners Sugar**
1	**Can Sweetened Condensed Milk** (14 ounce)
1	**Can Coconut** (3½ ounce)
1	**Teaspoon Vanilla**
1	**Stick Butter, Melted**
4	**Cups Pecans, Chopped**
12	**Ounce Package Semi-Sweet Chocolate Chips**
	Paraffin (1½ x 2½ Slab)

Mix sugar, milk, coconut and vanilla together. Mix butter and pecans together. Add pecans to sugar mixture, mix thoroughly (by hand). Form into small balls, chill or freeze until completely cold. Melt chocolate chips and paraffin together in top of a double boiler. Insert a toothpick into cold candy balls, dip balls into melted chocolate, coating balls completely, place on waxed paper, remove toothpick, cool until chocolate has set. Store in air tight container in refrigerator or freeze.

Sugar Peanuts

2   **Cups Raw Peanuts** (with skins)
1   **Cup Sugar**
½   **Cup Water**

Combine sugar and water in a heavy pot, cook over medium heat until sugar dissolves turning into a syrup. Add peanuts and continue cooking, stirring frequently, until syrup starts to sugar, forming sugar crystals on peanuts. When peanuts are completely coated with sugar crystals and no syrup is left in pan pour onto an ungreased cookie sheet that has been lined with foil. Spread so that peanuts are separated. Bake at 300 degrees for about 15 to 20 minutes, stirring every five minutes or so to keep peanuts separated. Cool completely, seal in air tight container.

Pecan Frogs

1   **Egg White**
¾   **Cup Light Brown Sugar**
½   **Teaspoon Vanilla Flavoring**
1½   **Cups Pecan Halves**

Beat egg white until stiff, add brown sugar and flavoring, mixing well, add pecan halves. Spoon out one pecan half at a time onto a greased baking sheet. Bake at 300 degrees about 10 to 15 minutes until golden brown.

Chocolate Fudge

7	Tablespoons Butter
9	Tablespoons Cocoa
½	Cup Light Corn Syrup
1	Teaspoon Vanilla Flavoring
1	Tablespoon Water
1	Pound 10x Powdered Sugar
⅓	Cup Instant Nonfat Dry Milk
½	Cup Chopped Nuts

Melt butter in top of double boiler, add cocoa, mix well. Gradually stir in corn syrup, flavoring and water. Sift powdered sugar and instant milk together, add to chocolate mixture until blended, smooth, and slightly shiny. Remove from heat, add nuts and pour into buttered dish. Cool.

Microwave Chocolate Fudge

½   **Cup Butter**
1   **Pound Box 10X Powdered Sugar**
½   **Cup Cocoa**
¼   **Cup Milk**
1   **Teaspoon Vanilla Flavoring**
½   **Cup Nuts, Chopped**

Melt butter in microwave, add sugar, cocoa, and milk. Mix well then microwave on high for 2 minutes, stirring every 30 seconds. Add flavoring and nuts, stir vigorously until smooth. Pour into glass baking dish, freeze or refrigerate until firm.

Divine Divinity

2½ **Cups Sugar**
½   **Cup Light Corn Syrup**
½   **Cup Water**
¼   **Teaspoon Salt**
2   **Egg Whites**
1   **Teaspoon Vanilla**
½   **Cup Chopped Nuts** (optional)

In a heavy 2 quart saucepan, pour together sugar, corn syrup, water, and salt, trying to keep sugar off sides of pan. Clip candy thermometer to side of pan (for perfect divinity, thermometer is best investment). Cook and stir gently over medium-high heat until sugar dissolves. Try to avoid splashing syrup on sides of pan. Cook, without stirring, to 260 degrees or hard-ball stage. Remove from heat. Immediately, in a large bowl, beat egg whites at high speed of electric mixer until stiff peaks are formed.

Remove the thermometer from syrup, gradually pour hot syrup in a thin stream over egg whites,

DIVINE DIVINITY *(continued)*

_____

beating at high speed. Add syrup slowly. Add vanilla, beat at high speed of mixer for 4 to 5 minutes, until candy holds its shape when beaters are lifted out (mixture will fall in a ribbon, but will mound on itself.) Stir in chopped nuts, if desired. Quickly drop by teaspoonfuls onto waxed paper.

If candy flattens out, beat another ½ to 1 minute more. If candy is too thick and surface is rough, beat in a few drops of hot water at a time until candy is softer consistency.

Granny's Chocolate Clusters Peanuts

5   Cups Raw Or Green Peanuts

Spread raw shelled peanuts in a single layer in a shallow baking pan. Place in a 300 degree oven for 30 to 45 minutes. Stir frequently until peanuts have browned very lightly and are completely toasted. Cool completely.

Chocolate Cluster
1   Pound Chocolate Bark
5   Cups Parched Peanuts

Melt chocolate bark in microwave, stirring every 20 to 30 seconds. Do not overcook, chocolate just needs to be melted completely. Add parched peanuts that have cooled to room temperature, stir coating peanuts completely with chocolate.

_____

Drop peanut/chocolate mixture on waxed paper using tablespoon. Cool on counter or in refrigerator until firm. Store in air tight container.

Submitted by: Ruth Youngblood (Granny to me)

Hay Stacks

2	**Cups Butterscotch Morsels**
4	**Tablespoons Peanut Butter**
6	**Ounces Chow Mien Noodles**
½	**Cup Roasted Peanuts**

Melt butterscotch morsels and peanut butter in microwave, stirring to prevent scorching. Add noodles and peanuts, mixing well. Drop by spoonfuls onto waxed paper, cool. Store in air tight container. Can substitute chopped toasted pecans for peanuts if desired.

Peanut Brittle

1½	**Cups Sugar**
½	**Cup White Corn Syrup**
2	**Tablespoons Water**
1½	**Teaspoons Butter**
2	**Cups Peanuts**
1	**Teaspoon Baking Soda**

Mix sugar, syrup, water and butter in a heavy saucepan, bring to a boil over medium high heat. Add peanuts, continue to boil 10 to 15 minutes on medium heat. Stir to prevent scorching. Remove from heat, add baking soda, stir until mixture turns a golden color. Pour on a greased cookie sheet, using a wooden spoon to spread hot brittle thinly. Let cool, break into pieces. Store in air tight container.

Forgotten Cookies

2	**Egg Whites, Beaten Stiff**
¾	**Cup Sugar**
1	**Teaspoon Vanilla Flavoring**
1	**Cup Pecans, Chopped**
1	**Package Chocolate Chips** (6 ounce)

Add sugar to egg whites that have been beaten stiff, beat well. Add vanilla. Fold in nuts and chocolate chips. Spoon onto a foil lined cookie sheet, place in a preheated 350 degree oven. Turn oven off, leave overnight.

Virginia's Teacake Cookies

2	**Cups Sugar**
1	**Cup Butter, Softened**
2	**Eggs**
4	**Cups Self-Rising Flour**
1	**Teaspoon Vanilla Flavoring**

Beat sugar and butter until fluffy. Add eggs, flour and flavoring, beat until smooth. Chill in refrigerator at least one hour. Remove half of dough at a time and roll out to $\frac{1}{4}^{th}$ inch on floured cloth. Cut with cookie cutters to desired shape. Bake in 400 degree oven for 5 to 8 minutes. Do not over cook, cookies do not need to be brown. Glaze cookies with powder sugar and water mixed to pouring consistency.

Mema's Cowboy Cookies

1	Cup Butter
1	Cup Sugar
1	Cup Brown Sugar
2	Eggs
1	Teaspoon Vanilla Flavoring
1	Teaspoon Baking Soda
2	Cups Plain Flour
½	Teaspoon Baking Powder
½	Teaspoon Salt
2	Cups Oatmeal, Uncooked
1	Cup Nuts, Chopped
1	Package Chocolate Chips (12 ounce)

Cream butter and sugar together. Add eggs to butter mixture one at a time, beating well, add flavoring. Sift dry ingredients together and add to mixture, beating until smooth. Stir in oatmeal, nuts and chocolate chips. Drop by teaspoonfuls, 2 inches apart on greased cookie sheet. Bake in 350 degree oven for 10 to 12 minutes, or until desired crispness.

Chocolate Chip Cookies

2½	Cups All-Purpose Flour
1	Teaspoon Baking Soda
¾	Cup Butter, Melted and Cooled
1½	Cups Brown Sugar
1	Egg
2	Teaspoons Vanilla Flavoring
1	Cup Semi-Sweet Chocolate Chips

Combine Flour and baking soda. In another bowl, combine melted butter and brown sugar, mixing well. Stir in egg and vanilla. Add flour mixture, stirring until combined. Stir in chocolate chips. Drop dough by spoonfuls onto cookie sheet covered with parchment paper, about two inches apart. Bake in a preheated 350 degree oven about 10 to 12 minutes.

This is very similar to the chocolate chip cookie recipe on the Blue Bonnet Margarine box – easy, good, and keeps well several days in the fridge.

Pecan Topped Grahams

¼ **Cup Butter**
½ **Cup Brown Sugar**
2 **Teaspoons White Corn Syrup**
½ **Cup Pecans, Chopped**
Whole Graham Crackers

Heat butter and sugar over low heat, just until butter is melted. Remove from heat, stir in corn syrup and pecans. Fill cookie sheet lined with parchment paper with a layer of Graham Crackers. Pour corn syrup and pecan mixture over top of crackers, spreading all over top and to edges of crackers. Bake crackers 5 to 6 minutes in a preheated 350 degree oven. Remove from heat, cool, break into squares. Store tightly covered.

Shoney's Style Strawberry Pie

2	Cups Strawberries
1	Cup Sugar
3	Tablespoons Cornstarch
3	Tablespoons Strawberry Jell-O
1	Cup Hot Water
1	Frounceen Pie Crust (9 inch), Baked and Cooled

Mix sugar and cornstarch. Add hot water, cook, stirring frequently, over low heat until thick. Add Jell-O, stirring until dissolved. Add strawberries, stirring gently to coat completely. Pour into baked pie crust — chill before serving. Garnish with whipped cream.

Buttermilk Pie

3	Eggs
1	Cup Sugar
2	Tablespoons Flour
½	Cup Butter, Melted
1	Cup Buttermilk
½	Teaspoon Vanilla Flavoring
½	Teaspoon Lemon Flavoring
1	Frounceen Pie Crust (9 inch), Unbaked

Combine eggs, sugar, flour and butter. Mix in lemon flavoring, vanilla, and buttermilk. Pour into unbaked frozen pie shell. Bake at 350 degrees for 45 minutes.

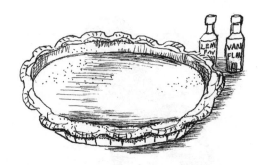

Japanese Fruit Pie

1	Cup Butter, Melted
12	Ounces Milk Chocolate Chips
2	Cups Sugar
5	Eggs, Beaten
1	Cup Coconut
1	Cup Pecans, Chopped
1	Teaspoon Vanilla Flavoring

Heat butter and chocolate chips over low heat until completely melted. Remove from heat, stir in sugar and beaten eggs. Add remaining ingredients, mixing well. Pour into two unbaked pie shells. Bake in a 350 degree preheated oven for about 30 minutes.

Chocolate Delight

Step 1: Crust
- 1   **Cup Flour**
- ½   **Cup Butter, Melted**
- ½   **Cup Pecans, Chopped**

Combine all ingredients in step 1 – pat into bottom of a 9 x 13 inch baking dish. Bake at 350 degrees for 15 minutes. Cool completely.

Step 2: Filling:
- 1   **Cup Whipped Topping**
- 1   **Cup Powdered Sugar**
- 8   **Ounce Cream Cheese, Softened**

Mix all ingredients in Step 2 – spread on cooled crust.

CHOCOLATE DELIGHT (continued)

Step 3: Topping:

- **3**   **Cups Cold Milk**
- **2**   **Small** (3 ounce) **Packages Chocolate Instant Pudding [or 1 Large** (5.9 ounce) **Package]**

Stir instant pudding and milk together, mix well. Pour over filling, garnish with additional whipped topping and mini chocolate chips.

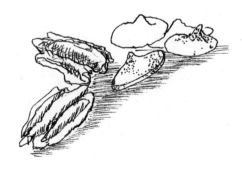

Chocolate Cherry Dessert

2	**Packages Whipped Topping** (*12 ounce*)
1	**Can Cherry Pie Filling** (*20 ounce*)
1	**Large Package Chocolate Cream Filled Cookies, Crumbled**

Cover bottom of a trifle bowl with whipped topping. Then layer crumbled cookies, whipped topping, and ½ cherry pie filling. Repeat. Top with whipped topping garnished with chocolate cookie crumbs. Refrigerate several hours before serving.

Egg Custard

1 1/4   **Cups Sugar**
2   **Tablespoons Flour**
3   **Eggs, Beaten**
1/2   **Cup Butter, Melted**
1/4   **Cup Buttermilk**
1   **Frounceen Pie Crust (8 inch), Unbaked**
Pinch of Salt

Combine flour and sugar together. Add eggs and butter, mix well. Stir in buttermilk and salt. Pour into unbaked pie shell and bake at 350 degrees for 20 to 25 minutes.

Doubleberry Cobbler

Pastry

3	**Cups Plain Flour**
1	**Teaspoon Salt**
1	**Cup Butter**
½	**Cup Ice Cold Water**

Sift flour and salt together. Add butter, blend until crumbly. Add ice water, sprinkling in slowly, while continuing to work with mixture, until dough forms. Divide dough into two balls, flatten out to form a disk, wrap each disk in plastic wrap, place in refrigerator overnight. Take dough out of refrigerator, let stand 30 minutes, roll out one dough disk to form a thin pastry, place in bottom of a 9 x 13 inch pan.

Filling:

6	**Cups Blackberries**
2	**Cups Blueberry Pie Filling**
½	**Cup Sugar**
1 ½	**Teaspoons Almond Extract**
¼-⅓	**Cup Butter**

Mix berries and pie filling, add sugar and extract, pour on top of crust. (add a little water to bowl to get all the berry filling in bowl, pour this over berry mixture.) Dot mixture with butter. Roll second pastry disk out to about ⅛ inch to ¼ inch thick — cut into strips, place strips on top of berry mixture. Bake in 400 degree preheated oven about 30 minutes, until crust is golden brown.

Mrs. Sparkman, from Sparkman's Dairy in Colquitt County, cooked this on one of the Cooking With Hugh shows, it was wonderful, especially topped with Sparkman's Ice Cream.

Coconut Pie

3	Eggs, Beaten
1½	Cups Sugar
½	Cup Butter, Melted
1	Tablespoon Vinegar
1	Teaspoon Vanilla Flavoring
1	Can Coconut (8 ounce)
1	Frounceen Pie Crust (8 inch), Unbaked

Mix butter, beaten eggs, sugar, vinegar and flavoring together. Stir in coconut. Pour into frozen unbaked pie shell. Bake at 350 degrees for about 1 hour.

Amazing Coconut Pie

2	**Cups Milk**
¾	**Cup Sugar**
½	**Cup Biscuit Mix**
4	**Eggs, Beaten**
¼	**Cup Butter**
1 ½	**Teaspoons Vanilla Flavoring**
1	**Cup Flaked Coconut**

Combine milk, sugar, biscuit mix, eggs, butter and vanilla. Mix well, beat for 3 minutes on low speed. Pour into a greased 9 inch pie pan. Sprinkle top of pie with the coconut, bake at 350 degrees for 35 to 40 minutes. Serve warm.

Coconut and Pineapple Pie

5   **Eggs, Beaten**
2   **Cups Sugar**
½   **Cup Butter, Melted**
2   **Cups Coconut**
1   **Can Crushed Pineapple** (8 ounce), **Drained**
1   **Teaspoon Vanilla Flavoring**

Mix all ingredients together, pour into 2 unbaked pie shells, bake at 350 degrees for about 25 to 30 minutes.

Fried Fruit Pies

1   **Bag Dried Fruit** *(Peaches or Apples)*
2   **Cups Water**
1   **Cup Sugar**
½   **Teaspoon Cinnamon**
6   **Biscuits, Uncooked Flour**
Cooking Oil

Combine dried fruit, sugar, cinnamon and water, cook on low heat until fruit is tender. Drain. On a flour covered cloth or waxed paper, roll out each biscuit into a thin round disk (can use canned or frozen biscuits that have been thawed) fill one side of each circle with fruit, leaving about ½ inch edge of dough free of fruit. Fold over other side of dough and seal edges with a fork. Dredge each in flour, fry in hot oil in a large heavy skillet until both sides are golden brown. Drain, sprinkle with powdered sugar if desired.

Grilled Peaches

6-8 **Firm, Ripe Peaches**
¾ **Cup Pineapple Juice**
¼ **Cup Brown Sugar**
1 **Teaspoon Lemon Juice**
¼ **Teaspoon Cinnamon**

Combine all ingredients, except peaches, in a large baggie or shallow dish. Cut peaches in halves, leaving skin on, but remove seed — place in juice mixture. Marinate in refrigerator about 30 minutes, turning once or twice to coat peaches, well. Grill peaches over medium heat, cut side down on greased rack with lid closed, for about five minutes on each side or until golden. Serve with ice cream sprinkled with cinnamon. Could also make kabobs with pineapple, peaches, cherries using this same marinade recipe.

Lemon Creme Pie

1   **Can Sweetened Condensed Milk**
    (14 ounce)
1   **Can Frounceen Lemonade** *(12 ounce)*
1   **Container Whipped Topping**
    (8 ounce)
1   **Graham Cracker Crust**

Mix softened, but not thawed lemonade with condensed milk. Fold in whipped topping, spoon into cracker crust. Chill overnight (can freeze).

Lemon Ice Box Pie

1   **Can Sweetened Condensed Milk**
       (14 ounce)
3   **Egg Yolks**
Juice Of 3 Lemons (about ½ cup)
1   **Graham Cracker Crust**

Beat condensed milk, egg yolks and lemon juice together until thickened. Pour into a graham cracker pie crust.

Meringue
3   **Egg Whites**
⅓   **Cup Sugar**

Beat egg whites until stiff, add sugar continuing to beat. When smooth and stiff, spread on top of lemon pie, bake in a 350 degree oven for 10 to 15 minutes, just until meringue has browned. Refrigerate at least 3 hours before serving.

Lemon Squares

Crust

1	**Box Lemon Supreme Cake Mix** (18¼ ounce)
½	**Cup Shortening**
1	**Teaspoon Lemon Flavoring**
2	**Eggs**

Mix all ingredients, should form a ball of dough, press dough in bottom of 9 x 13 inch baking pan.

Top

8	**Ounce Cream Cheese, Softened**
2	**Teaspoons Lemon Flavoring**
1	**Pound Box 10x Powdered Sugar**
2	**Eggs**

Combine all ingredients, pour over dough crust. Bake in 325 degree oven for about 45 to 50 minutes.

Can substitute orange cake mix for lemon cake mix, very good, too. If you use orange cake mix be sure to use orange flavoring instead of lemon.

Lemon Brownies

1	**Box Lemon Supreme Cake Mix** (18¼ ounce)
½	**Cup Sugar**
2-3	**Tablespoons Water**
½	**Cup Oil**
2	**Eggs**

Mix all ingredients together, spread into a 9 X 13 inch baking pan, bake at 350 degrees for about 20 to 30 minutes, or until pick inserted in middle comes out clean.

Can frost with a thin cream cheese frosting.

½	**Cup Butter, Softened**
1	**Package Cream Cheese,** (8 ounce) **Softened**
1	**Pound Powdered Sugar**
1	**Teaspoon Lemon Flavoring**

Beat butter and cream cheese at medium speed with an electric mixer until creamy. Gradually add powdered sugar, beating at low speed until blended; stir in lemon flavoring. May need to add a tablespoon of milk to reach desired consistency.

Peach Cobbler

3   **Cups Sliced Peaches**
1   **Cup Sugar**
1   **Cup Milk Or Buttermilk**
1   **Cup Self-Rising Flour**
½   **Cup Butter**

Mix sugar, flour and milk together. Melt butter in bottom of a greased baking dish. Layer peaches in butter, pour flour/sugar/milk mixture over peaches. Bake in preheated 350 degree oven about 45 minutes. Wonderful served with vanilla ice cream.

Peanut Butter Pie

1	**Package Cream Cheese** (8 ounce), **Softened**
1	**Container Whipped Topping** (12 ounce)
1	**Cup Peanut Butter, Smooth or Crunchy**
1	**Cup Powdered Sugar, Sifted**
3	**Tablespoons Milk**
1	**Graham Cracker Pie Crust** (9 inch)

Beat cream cheese until fluffy, add whipped topping, peanut butter, sugar and milk. Beat well. Spoon in cracker crust and chill at least 5 to 6 hours before serving. Garnish with peanuts and additional whipped topping, if desired. Also good in a chocolate cookie crumb pie crust and/or with chocolate chunks added to filling.

Pecan Pie

6	**Eggs**
1½	**Cups Light Corn Syrup**
1½	**Cups Sugar**
1	**Tablespoon Flour**
4	**Tablespoons Butter, Melted**
2	**Teaspoons Vanilla Flavoring**
1	**Teaspoon Salt**
2	**Cups Pecans, Halves or Chopped**
2	**Frounceen Deep Dish Pie Shells, Unbaked**

Beat eggs slightly, add syrup, sugar, butter, flour, flavoring, and salt to beaten eggs. Mix well, stir in pecans. Pour into unbaked pie shell, bake at 350 degrees for 45 to 50 minutes.

Banana Pudding

1   **Large Package Vanilla Instant Pudding** *(5.9 ounce)*

1   **Package Lemon Instant Pudding** *(3 ounce)*

5   **Cups Milk**

1   **Container Whipped Topping** *(12 ounce)*

1   **Cup Sour Cream**

4   **Ripe Bananas**

1   **Box Vanilla Wafers** *(12 ounce)*

Mix pudding mixes and milk. Fold in about half of whipped topping and all of the sour cream. Place layer of vanilla wafers in dish, topped with layer of sliced bananas. Pour half of pudding mixture over bananas. Repeat with layer of wafers, bananas and remaining pudding mixture. Top with remaining whipped topping. Refrigerate.

Sweet Potato Pie

4	Medium Sweet Potatoes, Boiled
1	Cup Sugar
½	Cup Butter
½	Cup Milk
2	Eggs
1	Teaspoon Vanilla Flavoring
1	Teaspoon Cinnamon
1	Frounceen Pie Shell (9 inch), Unbaked

Mash or beat cooked sweet potatoes until smooth, add sugar, butter, and milk. Blend well, adding flavoring, eggs, and cinnamon. Pour into unbaked pie shell, bake at 350 degrees for 30 to 35 minutes.

Ambrosia

10-12 Oranges
½-1 Cup Coconut
½   Cup Pecans, Chopped
Small Jar Cherries (8 - 10 ounce), **Halved**

Peel oranges, make sure that white pith is removed. Cut orange sections into large chunks. Mix oranges, coconut, pecans and cherries. May need to add extra orange juice. Chill, serve.

Southern Fried Happiness

6	Frozen Southern-Style Biscuits, Thawed or 1 Can Southern-Style Biscuits
1	Cup Powdered Sugar
2	Tablespoons Cinnamon
1	Cup Fruit Preserves
Ice Cream	
3	Cups Cooking Oil

Cut biscuits into quarters and drop into hot grease. Fry for 3 to 4 minutes or until golden brown. Remove from grease and drain on paper towels. Combine sugar and cinnamon. Roll biscuits in sugar mixture to coat.

Heat fruit preserves in microwave safe dish on high for 1 minute, or until soupy.

Serve biscuits in bowl topped with ice cream and melted fruit preserves. Really good with Strawberry-Fig Preserves on page 29. For breakfast, try serving without ice cream and preserves. Tastes like powdered sugar donut holes!!

Snicker Pie

4	**King Size Snicker Bars**
½	**Cup Peanut Butter**
1½	**Tablespoons Half And Half**
4	**Cups Cool Whip**
4	**Ounces Cream Cheese**
1	**Deep Dish Graham Cracker Pie Crust**

In double boiler, melt together Snicker bars, peanut butter, half and half, and cream cheese. Fold in Cool Whip. Pout into crust and freeze 4 to 6 hours.

Beverages, Microwave and Miscellaneous

Index

Favorite Recipes:

Title   Page Number

_____

_____

_____

_____

_____

_____

_____

_____

_____

_____

_____

_____

_____

_____

Hot Chocolate Powder

16	Ounces Nestle Quick
8	Quart Size Powdered Milk
2	Cups Powdered Sugar
11	Ounces Non-Dairy Creamer

Mix all ingredients together. Store in air tight container. Stir 2 tablespoons of mix into cup of hot water. Garnish with marshmallows or a peppermint stick.

This also makes a great gift — fill pint jars with mix, decorate lid, add mixing directions.

Afternoon Refresher

6   **Scoops Vanilla Ice Cream**
1   **Cup Orange Juice**
2   **Tablespoons Honey**

Put ice cream, orange juice, and honey in blender.
Mix well, garnish with orange slice.

Southern Style Sweet Tea

2-3   **Quarts Water**
1   **Family Size Tea Bag**
1   **Cup Sugar**

Heat 3 cups of water with tea bag in a microwave safe pitcher in microwave for 5 to 6 minutes, do not boil. Let tea water steep for 6 to 10 minutes. Remove tea bag, add sugar and remaining water to fill pitcher, stir until sugar has dissolved. Chill. Serve over ice. Water and sugar should be adjusted to suit taste.

Spiced Cider

---

2   **Quarts Apple Cider**
1   **Bag Cinnamon Red Hearts**
     (4-6 ounce)

Combine cider and cinnamon red hearts in a crock pot. Heat on high for one hour, stirring occasionally to make sure that red hearts are melted. Turn heat to low. Serve garnished with a cinnamon stick (smells great).

Microwave Fudge

- ½ **Cup Butter**
- 1 **Pound Box 10x Powdered Sugar**
- ½ **Cup Cocoa**
- ¼ **Cup Milk**
- 1 **Teaspoon Vanilla Flavoring**
- ½ **Cup Nuts, Chopped**

Melt butter in microwave, add sugar, cocoa, and milk. Mix well then microwave on high for 2 minutes, stirring every 30 seconds. Add flavoring and nuts, stir vigorously until smooth. Pour into glass baking dish, freeze or refrigerate until firm.

Chicken Divan

2	**Package Frozen Broccoli** (10 ounce), **Cooked**
2	**Cups Chicken or Turkey, Cooked & Chopped**
2	**Cans Cream of Chicken Soup** (10 ¾ ounce)
½	**Cup Mayonnaise**
½	**Tablespoon Lemon Juice**
½	**Teaspoon Curry Powder**
½	**Cup Cheddar Cheese, Grated**
½	**Cup Bread Crumbs**
1	**Tablespoon Butter**

Cook frozen broccoli about 6 to 8 minutes in microwave on high, stirring every 2 minutes. Place cooked broccoli in microwave safe baking dish. Layer cooked and chopped chicken or turkey over broccoli. Combine cream of chicken soup, mayonnaise, lemon juice and curry powder. Spread over chicken. Mix cheese, butter and bread crumbs together, sprinkle over mayonnaise mixture. Cook in microwave on high for 12 minutes, turning dish quarter turn every 3 or 4 minutes.

Taco Seasoning

1	**Tablespoons Chili Powder**
2	**Teaspoons Onion Powder**
1	**Teaspoon Ground Cumin**
1	**Teaspoon Garlic Powder**
1	**Teaspoon Paprika**
1	**Teaspoon Oregano**
1	**Teaspoon Sugar**
½	**Teaspoon Salt**

Mix all ingredients together, this makes 3 tablespoons seasoning mix, which is equal to a ¼ ounce package of commercial seasoning.

If you are from the South, or wish you were, there is nothing as good as boiled peanuts, fried peanuts, parched peanuts, toasted peanuts, or raw peanuts straight from the field. Hope you enjoy these basic peanut recipes!

Fried Peanuts

Heat deep fryer to 375 degrees. Place shelled peanuts in hot oil for 4 minutes. Remove peanuts from boiling oil, drain on paper towels. Spread peanuts out, sprinkle with salt. ENJOY!

Boiled Peanuts

2–3 Pounds Raw ("Green") Peanuts
½–1 Cup Salt

After picking the peanuts from the vines, wash them at least 3 or 4 times, draining the water after each washing. Since peanuts are grown underground, they have a great deal of dirt on them, so wash really well to remove all the grit. After peanuts have been washed, place in a large pot (6-8 quart size) with enough water to cover the peanuts. Add salt, bring water to a boil over high heat. Cover, reduce the heat to medium, slow boil for about 4 hours or until peanuts are tender, stirring occasionally. May need to keep adding water to keep peanuts covered and may need to add more salt. Taste peanuts and salt them as needed, because boiled peanuts are supposed to taste salty.

When the peanuts are tender, remove from heat and let stand in salted water for about an hour. Drain, then serve warm.

May store boiled peanuts in refrigerator for 3 or 4 days or may even freeze them. Best eaten warm, so will need to warm them slightly in the microwave for a few minutes before eating if frozen or refrigerated.

Of course the best peanuts are the ones that you buy directly from the farmer straight from his field. But you can purchase raw peanuts in the produce section of your local grocery store. If you do that, you will need to wash them really well and soak the peanuts for at least 8 hours before boiling. Boiling time will probably need to be adjusted also, because the drier the peanuts, the longer it will take them to become tender.

Toasted Peanuts

Place a small amount of peanut oil in a shallow pan, pour peanuts into oil, stir them until they are coated (there should not be any excess oil in pan), peanuts should just have an oily surface. Bake peanuts in a preheated 350 degree oven for 20 minutes. Stir often so they will bake and brown evenly. Spread peanuts out on paper towels to drain any excess oil, then sprinkle them lightly with salt, if desired.

Cooking With Hugh

In Measuring, Remember...

3 Teaspoons = 1 Tablespoon

2 Tablespoons = ⅛ Cup

4 Tablespoons = ¼ Cup

8 Tablespoons = ½ Cup

12 Tablespoons = ¾ Cup

16 Tablespoons = 1 Cup

4 Ounces = ½ Cup

8 Ounces = 1 Cup

2 Cups = 1 Pint

2 Pints = 1 Quart

1 Quart = 4 Cups

1 Pound Butter = 2 Cups or 4 Sticks

Pinch = as much as can be taken between tip of finger and thumb.

16 Ounces = 1 Pound

Substitutions:

1 Whole Egg = 2 Egg Yolks, plus 1 Tablespoon water (for custard recipes omit water)

1 Cup Granulated Sugar = 1 ⅓ Cups Brown sugar or 1 ½ Cups Powdered Sugar

1 ¾ Cups Confectioners Sugar = 1 Cup Granulated Sugar, packed

1 Cup Brown Sugar = 1 Cup Granulated Sugar plus 2 Tablespoons Molasses

1 Cup Corn Syrup = ⅔ Cup Granulated Sugar plus ⅓ Cup Water

1 Pound Cornmeal = 3 Cups

1 Lemon Rind = 1 Tablespoon Grated Rind

1 Orange Rind = 2 Tablespoons Grated Rind

3 – 4 Medium Oranges = 1 Cup

1 Tablespoon Fresh Herb = ⅓ to ½ Teaspoon Dried Herb (same herb)

1 Clove Garlic = ⅛ Teaspoon Garlic Powder

15 Graham Crackers = 1 Cup Crumbs

23 Saltine Crackers = 1 Cup Crumbs

¾ Cup Cracker Crumbs = 1 Cup Bread Crumbs

Index

Meats, Gravies and Main Dishes

Salads, Salad Dressings, Sauces, Glazes and Soups

"Special Thanks" from Hugh

I first want to thank God for giving me life and for blessing me beyond my greatest imagination. My three children, Ivey, Brady, and Brittney, who each hold a very special place in my heart. My Mom and Dad for loving me even though I haven't always been perfect. My grandparents for sharing their strengths, guidance, and wisdom with me. My brothers and sister for being a part of my life. Debbie S. for being such a great Christian friend and always willing to give me good advice. Rooster, Cari, Eric, WALB-TV, and the rest of the "Cooking With Hugh" production staff. My staff at Carroll's Sausage & Meats for their hard work and friendship. My dear friends for always listening to my wild and crazy ideas and all those who pray for me. May God bless you. Hope you enjoy this cookbook.

Hugh A. Hardy, Jr.

To order additional copies, make checks payable to:
Father & Son Publishing, Inc. and mail to:
4909 North Monroe Street • Tallahassee, Florida 32303

Please send me _____ copies of **Cooking with Hugh** @ $19.95 plus $3.00 each for postage and handling. Florida residents add 7% sales tax.
Enclosed is my check or money order for $ _____

Name _____

Address _____

City_____ State _____ Zip _____

MasterCard/Visa Card # _____CV Code_____

Exp. date _____ Signature _____

— —

To order additional copies, make checks payable to:
Father & Son Publishing, Inc. and mail to:
4909 North Monroe Street • Tallahassee, Florida 32303

Please send me _____ copies of **Cooking with Hugh** @ $19.95 plus $3.00 each for postage and handling. Florida residents add 7% sales tax.
Enclosed is my check or money order for $ _____

Name _____

Address _____

City_____ State _____ Zip _____

MasterCard/Visa Card # _____CV Code_____

Exp. date _____ Signature _____

— —

To order additional copies, make checks payable to:
Father & Son Publishing, Inc. and mail to:
4909 North Monroe Street • Tallahassee, Florida 32303

Please send me _____ copies of **Cooking with Hugh** @ $19.95 plus $3.00 each for postage and handling. Florida residents add 7% sales tax.
Enclosed is my check or money order for $ _____

Name _____

Address _____

City_____ State _____ Zip _____

MasterCard/Visa Card # _____CV Code_____

Exp. date _____ Signature _____

— —